Dear Reader,

This book defines spiritual as an understanding and acceptance of the fact that a power greater than ourselves controls the Universe and everything in it, including us. It sees the Universe as interconnected with all elements affecting each other and all being essential, though different.

Therefore; we are not in control, there is no hierarchy, and all elements are to be valued. Applied to management, these spiritual principles dictate an entirely new relationship between members of a workforce aimed at accomplishing a common objective; an approach we call The Spiritual Style of Management.

My personal experiences and thoughts are shared and pertinent literature is reviewed to help in exploring this concept. I needed a management philosophy reflecting my spiritual journey to guide my teaching and found one which guides all my relationships. You need to determine whether or not it makes sense for you.

Enjoy.

James F. McMichael, Ph.D.

The
SPIRITUAL
Style of
MANAGEMENT:

WHO IS RUNNING
THIS SHOW ANYWAY?

James F. McMichael, Ph.D.
SPIRIT FILLED PRESS, INC.
Havana, Florida

SPIRIT FILLED PRESS, INC.

2084 Tallavana Trail
Havana, Florida 32333

COPYRIGHT© 1996 BY JAMES F. McMICHAEL
We want you to use this book. But we do reserve all rights.
Contact us if you need to use any portion of the book.

MANUFACTURED IN THE UNITED STATES OF AMERICA

1 0 9 8 7 6 5 4 3 2 1

LIBRARY OF CONGRESS CATALOGING IN PUBLICATION DATA

McMICHAEL, JAMES F.

THE SPIRITUAL STYLE OF MANAGEMENT / JAMES F. McMICHAEL

1. MANAGEMENT 2. SPIRITUAL LIFE 3. BUSINESS 4. NEW AGE MOVEMENT 5. JAMES F.
McMICHAEL 1. TITLE

ISBN# 0-9656668-0-8

SPIRIT FILLED PRESS
provides a means for inspired writers to communicate with the world about them.
For information, write the above address or fax 904-539-3843

DEDICATION

To Jim, Scott, Julia and Steve…

"Your children are not your children.
They are the sons and daughters of Life's longing for itself."
The Prophet.

May Life be fully experienced in you on your spiritual journey.

TABLE OF CONTENTS

Page

ACKNOWLEDGMENTS

"No man is an island," said John Donne and that is so true when it comes to putting together a book like this. So many contributed so much, but here are a few I particularly want to thank.

To those who came before in their spiritual quest and in their search for a better way to manage, I owe my beginnings and my focus; the many authors whose work I have briefly reviewed here in the hopes that the reader will continue to search out and read the substantial literature available to those seeking the better way; and to those millions who work 12-step programs to find a spiritual solution to today's living problems and their founders who wrote the book, *Alcoholics Anonymous.*

To Sue Early and Dan Kimel who provided early editing and urged me on; Grantham Couch who painstakingly read and reread the manuscript providing objective insight; my students who kept after me to finish when it seemed overwhelming; Valerie Anthony who did final editing and suggested some major additions to the book; Linda Zingale who typed and retyped ad nauseam the drafts; my wife, Eileen, who provided important finishing touches; and to Julia, my daughter, who many years ago saw this book in me, even when I didn't see much in myself.

Finally, and most important, to God, my higher power, who inspired and directed this work. After being challenged by one of my students to write a book of this nature, I awoke in the morning and within fifteen minutes wrote down the title, and the title of most of the chapters. The first draft took only three weeks to write. Stephen

Covey came to town, took the rough draft and shared valuable insights with me on his experience in writing a book like this. Those "coincidences," that continuous stream of inspiration, "chance" meetings with authors or those in the book business who so generously shared information and helpful hints on how to proceed, all make it clear to me I am not running this show. I need only be open and I will be shown what to do.

PREFACE

This is a book about management, about forging a spiritual path towards a more humanistic — and productive — style of managing. It proposes to share with the reader ideas and experiences which are aimed at getting results through and with others. It is a highly personal discussion of my beliefs and the experiences that led to their creation. They are chronicled here in the hope that they may be useful to those who also see themselves on a spiritual journey while making their way through the work-a-day world.

There are many good management books out today. I not only enjoy reading them but use them to teach my classes.

So why this book?

The difference between this and other books on management is the concept of who is in charge. Time after time what comes across in books on management style is the concept that we managers — the holders of power, the anointed few — need to use certain techniques to get the employees to do what we have determined they should do. I have problems with that. We need direction in our organizations, but as a manager I do not believe I am any more powerful or anointed or competent than anyone else. I possess skills and talents, that is true. But so does everyone. Those gifts and talents may vary, but they all have value.

The true power, the true anointed one, the real giver of benefits and facts and information — in short, everything I need — is not me or any other manager. It is a power greater than myself and it is that power that directs what needs to be done.

The vision I have is of an organization which resembles a community of believers directed by one unifying force which the members both individually and collectively intuit.

As a manager, I am nothing more (or less) than a conduit through which that power can work. And that power works not only through me but through each and every employee in that organization. As a manager, my role, as compared with others, is more in articulating and focusing the direction that power seems to be giving us.

How do you accomplish organizational goals without running the show? That's what this book is all about. And while this style of management may sound more difficult than the top down, tell 'em what they need to know and make sure they do it approach, you will find in the long run it is much easier, more productive, and vastly more creative and successful because the organization is no longer limited to your personal power but expanded to an infinite power, a power which cares about you and will miraculously provide if you will just listen.

INTRODUCTION

There is considerable evidence of a huge spiritual movement in the world today.

While its roots go back to the beginning of civilization — Abraham, Plato, Confucius, Lao-Tzu, Buddha, Krishna, Muhammad, Jesus — the 20th century seems to have set the stage for a major spiritual thrust into the 21st century. Dr. Richard M. Bucke's 1901 book, *Cosmic Consciousness: a Study in the Evolution of the Human Mind,* tested his hypothesis that mankind is evolving into a new state. He sees:

> ...almost a member of a new species... an awareness of the life and order of the universe... an intellectual enlightenment... a state of moral exaltation... an indescribable feeling of elevation, elation, and joyousness... a quickening of the moral sense... a sense of immortality, a consciousness of eternal life... that he has already.[1]

His summary of many such individuals who had this spiritual evolutionary experience could be substantially added to in the last century.

In *The Book,* Bhagewan Shree Rajneesh describes a new age with growing momentum where "more and more people will be coming to recognize that something remains unfulfilled and has to be fulfilled." He sees an upheaval of human consciousness by the end of this century.[2]

Carl Gustav Jung, the Swiss psychoanalyst, is another who saw "the possibility that the human might evolve… into a being described better in fulfillment than in conflict terms… The shift in adulthood from material to spiritual concerns is part and parcel of the tendency to attain selfhood and integration."[3]

The point is, we seem to be in the midst of a spiritual revolution or renaissance as Mathew Fox would call it. And that revolution is spilling into the business as well as personal lives of many people. Evidence of interest in this field is seen in the cascade of newsletters, periodicals, and books with titles such as *Corporate Renaissance, The Reflective Executive, Inner Excellence* and *Seeds of Change*. A recent article entitled *"Conscious Business"* in the *Journal* cited visionary entrepreneur Paul Hawken in his recent Utne reader article where he estimated that 2,000 committed [to ethical and spiritual management] companies are generating annual combined sales of two billion dollars. The article goes on to state that "although the ethical business movement is not entirely the product of the West's recent turn toward a personal eclectic spirituality, the presence of that spirituality is clear and non-deniable." He further states that "…people who have arrived at a more spiritual work ethic have done so not because they couldn't succeed at conventional business but because their very success at 'business as usual' proved so unsatisfying and led them into more contemplative explorations."[4]

*   *   *

We are all familiar with the concept of management style, a consistent way of behaving as a manager based on certain beliefs, values, and assumptions about one's self and others. These styles have a direct impact on what and how results are obtained within an organization.

This book is about a new management style, what I call the Spiritual Style of Management. As a manager, I can recall my early training, the common wisdom given me about letting everyone know I was in charge, not explaining my orders, not fraternizing with the troops and the "need to know" communication system. It was based on a superior/subordinate top-down authoritarian mentality. And it felt good!! At least when I was the boss. You see, that style of management satisfied certain basic lower level needs, those of safety and security, dominance in the pecking order.

However, as I matured, other higher level needs became stronger, self actualization and a broader understanding of self in relation to others and the universe we inhabit. And, fortunately, new management paradigms became available to help me and others move towards fulfilling those needs. Participative management principles in Total Quality Management, coaching, systems based and other new approaches have opened the door for a new management paradigm. But still, the old top-down, superior/subordinate mentality comes out when we look at what is implied and actually done, even using these newer management styles.

We need to change our way of looking at management altogether. Not some new technique to improve productivity, but a basic overhaul of our relationships to each other in the work place. That is what this book is about, a spiritual style of management.

*   *   *

The concept of spirituality as used in this book refers to a set of beliefs concerning nature and the universe. These beliefs see a universal spirit, a higher power, a supreme energy source that was, is, and always will be and directs the flow of our universe and everything in it, including us. It has nothing to do with trances and Ouija boards. Nor is it about religion. Religion is a specific framework of beliefs, dogma, and credos that dictate a believer's faith and behavior. This book neither proposes a new religion nor argues with any existing religious bodies — or for that matter, non-religious bodies. What it proposes can fit within nearly any realistic belief system, whether it be secular or spiritual.

All those behavior guidance systems existing in our culture such as morals, norms, ethics, laws, as well as religions, are not to be discarded or ignored. Morals transmit our society's dominant values regarding certain forms of behavior. Ethics provide a logical way of reasoning through conflicts we may face in deciding what is appropriate behavior.

Laws and norms exist to try to move us from an alienated anarchistic mob to a conforming, authority-based society. I have no problem with any of those concepts.

However, I need some way to measure my use of those behavior-directing forces.

The "rule of thumb" is my spiritual guidance system, my belief in some universal spirit, some higher power, some supreme energy, and what it reveals to me as being appropriate for my behavior. This is not situational ethics. It is not willy-nilly choosing what feels good at the time without regard to consequences. It is a belief that within me lies some spark, some connection with that universal spirit and that my task is to be open to and directed by that inner voice. That voice is consistent over time and situations.

What this book proposes is that **the relationship of people to the universe places us in a perspective of subjects of that universe and not its controllers.** As Mathew Fox put it:

> The Cosmic Christ awakens mindfulness, which instructs persons in their need and right to experience the presence of divinity around and through them. It opens their minds and hearts to the universe, to what is and to where we are: citizens of a vast twenty-billion-year history that is still unfinished and which we are called to complete; citizens of a universe of one hundred billion galaxies, of which ours is a mysteriously small one.[5]

*   *   *

You will note many references to God in this book. Yet, I say this is not about religion. Well, then, why God with a capital G?

Let me try to explain lest you think I'm trying to somehow convert you to my particular view of God. My idea of God has changed many times in my life so far and will probably change some more. Having gone from agnostic to Catholic, I have known several different versions of God. Once, in a period of deep despair, I desperately sought solace, strength and direction. I found it in a tree.

Located in Maclay Gardens in Tallahassee, Florida, my tree, a towering, short-leafed pine, caught my attention one day as I was running. For some reason, I stopped running, walked up to the tree, put my arms as far as I could around its tremendous girth, and hugged it. An overwhelming sense of strength and peace came over me. I felt a tremendous surge of love for this mighty tree, and I hung on for what seemed like hours.

Finally, becoming aware I might look a little strange wrapped in an embrace with a tree, I stepped back and gazed in awe at its majestic branches reaching into the clear blue sky.

That tree was and is God speaking to me. It taught me many lessons through the years in which I continued to come and hug it, talk to it, just sit and be with it.

Today, I see God as the total energy source. God created, God directs. God is, was, and always will be. As the source of all energy, God allows me to tap into that energy if I so choose. If not, my Higher Power allows me to go my own way.

You see, I have no quarrel with whatever you perceive as God in your life, and all you need bring with you to the reading of this book is the sense that **there is a higher power and you are not it.** I do not believe in a randomly-directed universe. Like Einstein, I shall never believe that God plays dice with the universe. And, while it seems since time immemorial humankind has tried to become God, I am certain today I am not God, and I am content to be on a spiritual journey attempting to come close to that source that guides my life.

So, please allow me to use my word, God, and you use whatever word is best for you. God, as we all understand her/him/it in our own uniquely human way, will be able to communicate with us; of that much I am certain.

So, this spiritual journey inside myself and the power providing the direction for that journey is the basis for this book. Often I have found my own spiritual beliefs at odds with what I read and have taught in managerial courses. I believe there has to be a way to reconcile spiritual beliefs and managerial practices. This book outlines an approach to management based on spiritual principles, a system of management dealing with issues of control. I hope you find it useful. I know I have.

CHAPTER ONE

Spiritual Management: People And Principles

What is spiritual management? How is it different from other approaches to management? If it is different, how do you become a spiritual manager?

Several of those reading early drafts have strongly suggested that I provide some concrete material to help people understand and apply the principles outlined in this book. For me, this is a very difficult task. In the first place, you may presently be practicing spiritual management. Then, too, I see everyone on their own spiritual path who need to find their own way.

However, there appears to be certain principles or elements in the practice of spiritual management. Perhaps one way to approach this task is to identify some people I have worked for or with who strike me as individuals who used a spiritual style of management. By describing them and their behavior, we can perhaps then move to an understanding of more specific ways in which spiritual managers operate and from that the readers can create their own plan for adopting these principles in their management lives.

In thinking about all the managers I have known and worked closely with, only four came to mind as individuals who I would perceive as having most of the attributes of a spiritual manager. They are: Frank Pierce, my foreman at Fisher Body Division, General Motors Corp. in Lansing, Michigan, where I worked nights while at-

1

tending Michigan State during the day; Peretz (Perry) Katz, Executive Director of the Ingham County, Michigan, United Community Chest and Council, when I served as coordinator for the project on aging; Dr. Richard Bardwell, Chairman of the Wisconsin State Commission on Aging and former State Superintendent of Schools and former Director of the State Board of Vocational, Technical and Adult Education; and, finally, Anthony (Tony) Pearson, Senior Vice President of Unionmutual Life Insurance Company, responsible for strategic planning and organizational development and former General Manager of Scientific Methods, the managerial grid organization.

*   *   *

I worked for Frank Pierce at Fisher Body Division in the box car unloading dock from 1955 to 1957. Although only a junior in college, I was married and had one child, and was the sole provider for my family. Fisher Body made it possible for me to go to college by allowing me to work straight nights while everybody else was on a swing shift, working three weeks nights and three weeks days. As a result, I had the opportunity of working for two very different foremen.

Frank was one of the least controlling, yet motivating managers, for whom I ever worked. Yet, you would undoubtedly not consider the General Motors of this time to have advocated a spiritual style of management. The all-important goal of the organization was to keep the assembly line going and to make sure that cars got out the other end. How they got out wasn't as important as getting them out. It was high pressure, labor versus management, many long hours (I would work up to 16 hours straight and then go home, wash up and go to class). But it probably was not as bad as it was when my dad started working there many years before the union.

All the jobs were time studied. That is, there was a set time in which they were to be done and the manager's job was to make sure all the work got done on time and above all else, that the parts were there to keep the assembly line going. One of my two foremen was typical of the General Motors environment of the day. High pressure, constantly pacing up and down the dock, sticking his head in our car, making sure that we were doing our job, constantly chiding us to work faster to get the car out quicker. He was the epitome of the controlling manager. He didn't trust us and we didn't like him. We did our job and that was it. If he wanted anything extra, he was out of luck. He wasn't going to get it and, if he tried, we would call the union and file a grievance.

Frank, on the other hand, couldn't have been any more the opposite. When we would come in to work he would sit down, go over the list of cars that were available for unloading, look at the inventory he had on hand and we would agree on cars that needed to be unloaded so as to maintain a constant supply of parts into the assembly line. He would usually pair us with people who we could work with and where we could combine our strengths in order to get the job done quicker and easier. I remember my partner was another college student (we were the only two on the dock). Once he had determined that we had the skills necessary to unload the boxcar, he would pretty much leave us alone. We both knew how long we had to get the boxcar unloaded. Being inventive individuals like most workers on that dock, we could find ways to "beat the job" and get the car unloaded early. With Frank we would do that regularly because we knew he would still give us the allotted time to get the car unloaded. This meant that we could occasionally get an extra half hour or hour's worth of sleep in the back of the boxcar if we really hustled and got it mostly unloaded early in the evening. Frank never came by, never said a word, we got our job done, he got his parts, and we got a little nap. Everybody won. But the difference was that if there was an emergency and a car had to get out in order to get the parts for the line, all Frank had to do was to say, "Guys, we have a problem. We need to get this car out and we don't have as much time. If you can get it out for me, I would really appreciate it." We would get that car out. We would get the car out because we knew the next time that car had to be unloaded it would be allotted its regular time. Not the time we actually got it unloaded. We trusted Frank and we liked him. He trusted us and we always had the feeling he liked us, too.

Now many people would think Frank was lazy. You would see him sitting at his foreman's desk, feet up on the desk, maybe doing some reading, maybe chewing the fat with an inspector or a couple of guys who had their car in good shape. There always seemed to be sort of a relaxed atmosphere around the dock when Frank was the foreman. Even when we had a crisis and everybody pitched in to get the job done, there was a feeling like a smooth flowing team just really pushing and coming together to get the job done in a relaxed, confident kind of atmosphere, not pressured and harried or panicky. I can still remember some of the guys I worked with in that crew on that dock. I can't remember their names but I can see their faces. I can remember our conversations. It was a good feeling. We felt close together and confident in ourselves and in each other and in our abilities to get the job done. There wasn't a crew on that dock that couldn't and wouldn't beat the time if Frank asked them to. They were good people, good workers; we enjoyed each other and enjoyed our work experience there. I felt good about the work I did with Frank Pierce and I still look at some of those 1955, 1956, and 1957 Oldsmobiles I helped make, wondering which part I carried and how I contributed to making that car.

*   *   *

Perry Katz was Executive Director of the Ingham County United Community Chest and Council when I was hired as coordinator of its project on aging. I didn't start the project. There was a fellow that had been there before me. I came in with a background in public health and an acute awareness of the need to do something for the elderly, due in large part to the personal experience of watching my grandmother waste away and die with cancer, and my grandfather die because he had no reason to live. I still remember people saying, "Isn't it a blessing he finally died?" I thought about this man who had worked two jobs and raised 13 children. How proud and independent he had been, and I knew there was something wrong with our system that a man like that would end up being better off dead.

So I had lots of motivation to do something for the elderly and some background that would enable me to do it. Moreover, I was fortunate to have a wonderful advisory committee chaired by Dr. Fred Schwartz, Chairman of the American Medical Association Committee on Gerontology and a true mentor to me in that field. However, driven by my dislike of authority and high desire to act autonomously, I could have indeed had a difficult time with Perry had he been the typical controlling manager. But he wasn't.

I was the controller. The contrary employee who wanted to do his own thing. Be in charge. Run the show. Yet, Perry found a way to use my considerable skills by gently, yet firmly, giving me the direction I very badly needed in knowing how to work in a community organization setting. As Executive Director, Perry was a big deal in Lansing. He dealt directly with the most influential people in town — the head of the Oldsmobile Division for General Motors, the president of Motor Wheel, the president of Auto Owners Insurance Company. He could have easily seen himself as better than, higher than, more important than this lowly coordinator. But I never got that impression from him. His approach was always very low key. He was a very compassionate, caring person and I really felt that he genuinely cared about me as an individual and believed in me, in my ability to do something to help the elderly. He never really tried to tell me my business, but he would show me how to create a common vision for our project and mentor me when it came to the necessary skills of a community organizer. How to evaluate the strengths of the many volunteers I had to work with. How to structure the organization so as to achieve peak effectiveness from the many, many groups and committees we dealt with. How to develop the essential skills of social planning and to accomplish important social goals, not by building myself up, but by working with others in building them up so they got the credit and we all got the results we wanted. Perry would always remind me that I should keep my eye on the vision, on what it was we were trying to accomplish, and not be concerned with who gets credit for accomplishing it or who is actually "calling the shots." What was important was the vision, the goal of what we were there to do, and making sure it got accomplished by working with and through others over whom we had absolutely no authority.

His gentleness, caring and compassion didn't just affect me. It affected our whole organization. I remember we brought in a fund raiser from Philadelphia to head up the United Way Campaign. He was fairly aggressive and if we heard "back in Philadelphia" once we heard it a thousand times, but even this rather abrasive personality soon blended into our team. I will never forget the enjoyable social experiences and sharing in mutual support I felt with the staff there at the Ingham County Community Chest and Council. Sal Sagola, Paul Gezon, Bob Garrison, Bill Williams and, of course, my wonderful secretary, Lee, who gave me a Minute Maid orange juice can covered with white velvet with J.I.M. on it. I still have that can to this day. The sense of team, of unity, of cohesiveness, of mutual support that Perry created in that organization was very strong, yet he didn't try to be one of the guys. He created an atmosphere of support, mentored, taught and coached us. I never heard anyone complaining or bitching about the boss, about this lousy place to work even though, typical of the times, we were poorly paid. But we were social crusaders and we had somebody who believed in us, helped us, and supported us to help us accomplish those social visions we were striving to meet.

*   *   *

Dr. Bardwell, the only name I ever felt comfortable calling him, was Chairman of the Wisconsin State Commission on Aging. The Commission, a group of seven individuals appointed by the Governor and confirmed by the Wisconsin State Senate, had the responsibility for developing and overseeing the programs benefiting the elderly in the State of Wisconsin. It had broad powers and could have very easily become a political football. However, under Dr. Bardwell's leadership this organization was able to pull a diverse group of individuals together into a very effective, cohesive team, truly concerned with developing programs for Wisconsin's elderly. They used to say that we had three Democrats and three Republicans and one independent, and I am really not sure who was who. The point was, they really didn't care.

What they cared about was getting the job done. As its first executive director, I couldn't have asked for a better environment in which to work. Only 27 years old at the time, I brought with me tremendous drive to do something for the elderly, good organizational skills learned under Perry Katz and a tremendous amount of impatience. I saw established agencies like welfare as being more concerned with their fiefdoms than with actually doing anything for the elderly. I was chomping at the bit, always wanting to take them on. Fortunately, Dr. Bardwell was there to continuously give me counsel and direction. A strong but gentle man, he had a deep belief in the inherent goodness of people, including those bureaucrats I wanted to crucify. Former head of two different state agencies, he had a good understanding of the system and the way in which things get done in government. On our many automobile trips throughout the state to attend hearings (held on a regular basis for the elderly and for those working with the elderly to come and testify), he would listen quietly and patiently to me rattle on, and then make a few cogent comments, suggesting that being a little patient but continuing to work for our goals might work better than direct confrontation (which was my usual mode).

Beginning in 1962, the Commission held annual retreats where it would sequester itself in order to focus in-depth on the problems concerning the elderly and the need to develop long-range plans and strategies to implement those plans. We would emerge from those retreats fortified by a very good sense of where we were, where we needed to go and what we needed to do to get there, and all unified behind that mission. We had a conservative Republican industrialist and a liberal Democratic labor leader, a physician, a professor, a Jewish home administrator, a long-time farm activist leader and Dr. Bardwell. Well-connected politically and passionately committed to the elderly, Dr. Bardwell pulled this group together, not through force of his personality, but through his patience and wisdom. Believing in our inherent desire to benefit the elderly, he was willing to let our differences surface and be worked out.

As the agency's Executive Director, I was given considerable freedom in the development of the agency, its staff and programs. I was relied upon to develop our legislative proposals, our long-range plans, and our community assistance programs. The commission functioned as a real policy-making body because it had direction and perspective, which helped us become the effective agency we were. Memorable among our achievements was the passage of the first circuit breaker legislation in the nation granting property tax relief to the elderly through a system of income tax credits and refunds, the making of the first grant under the Older Americans Act and the develop-

ment of the prototype programs which became known as the Area
Agency on Aging under the United States Administration on Aging.
This was a highly productive time for me and as I looked at my
relationship with Dr. Bardwell it was one of mentor, guide, counselor, friend, and sounding board. He always made me feel like more,
not like less. I always felt he and the other commissioners had confidence in me and would support me in the efforts I put forth to carry
out the policies they had set. He has been dead many years now and
when I think of him I feel a sadness for not having him here to talk to
and to share with as I did those wonderful years with the State Commission on Aging.

*   *   *

Anthony Pearson was Executive Vice President of Unionmutual
Life Insurance Company and my office next door neighbor. Although
I technically worked with Tony and not for him, his position in our
company and my relative immaturity made our relationship more
mentor to student than co-workers. Tony came from Scientific Methods with whom we had worked in the development of our internal
managerial grid program which was the core management practice
of our organization. Ever a 9.9 manager, that is, one who has high
concern for people and high concern for results and uses team management as a way to accomplish those results, Tony helped me really
understand myself, my management style, and how to be effective in
large organizations. Always calm, always able to keep things in perspective as though he were somehow detached and could look at it
from a distance, Tony brought to me an appreciation of how a man-

ager could be tough, always striving for excellence, always striving for a way to do it better while at the same time building people up so they were capable of accomplishing the excellence that was being sought.

Like Perry, he had little concern for credit and much more concern for results. I can remember he used to have a little placard on his desk that said to the effect that it matters not who gets the credit but that the job gets done. Above all else, Tony always struck me as a person who was very happy in his own skin. He never seemed to need things outside of himself to make him whole or happy. He had a very close relationship with his wife and with a few others, but generally Tony wasn't someone you'd get close to. Though he was a very complete person, self-contained and available whenever you needed to talk to him, there wasn't any particular warmth or great amount of affection. Yet you felt that he really liked and valued you and valued his relationship with you; it just wasn't at a personal level. It was a business relationship and that was okay.

He and I both were members of the so-called top management team of the company, those who reported to the president, and I can remember well how he would keep us focused on our tasks or make sure that someone who perhaps had become quiet was given an opportunity to speak or that conflict was allowed to emerge and be dealt with effectively. While our president was a very effective person, I think his greatest strength was in recognizing the abilities of others and fully utilizing those abilities. Tony's strengths were fully utilized in our top management team meetings. One of his characteristics that caused me to select him as a spiritual manager was his sense of ethics, of rightness. The last time I spoke to him, he was writing a book and the second chapter had to do with business ethics.

I always felt that the people who worked for Tony felt free to express their opinions, to challenge existing ways in which things were done, to take risks and try new and different ways to accomplish better results. I never once heard him blame or place fault. He truly felt that everyone ought to have their "day in court" to present their ideas and to be listened to with respect. While a "facts, data and logic" oriented person, he never held himself out to be better than or higher than anybody else in the organization. His door truly was always open; he was always accessible to anyone, including me, for whom he had no administrative responsibility whatsoever.

When I think of his management style, I sigh a little inside because I realize that even as I have changed and grown I still have a ways to go to really be the kind of manager that Tony Pearson was. But then, that's today and there is always tomorrow. There is always opportunity for improvement.

*   *   *

Spiritual Management Principles

In preparing this book, it was suggested I use an approach similar to Stephen Covey's *Seven Habits of Highly Effective People* in order to come up with a list of characteristics of the spiritual manager.[1] To specify tools and techniques such a manager might employ is a difficult task. It is rather like giving a precise definition of love or God.

However, the following elements were generally present in the spiritual managers I have known and help frame this new workplace relationship – the spiritual style of management.

- **Control, the key issue.** As much as we might be encouraged to take charge, be in control of our lives, the spiritual manager knows at a gut level he is not running the show. Keeping all things in perspective, he sees the universe and all its creations as guided by a supreme being, a higher power, and realizes that power is also directing his work and that of those organizational members he serves as manager. Letting go of control is not difficult, he is not in control. Letting go of the illusion he is in control is difficult and has tremendous implications for all he does as a manager.

- **Vision, the key for unity and direction.** Able to see the big picture, the spiritual manager facilitates the shared vision of all her co-members. Not a mere statement, the vision is the compelling force driving all who belong to the work community.

- **Organizational simplicity.** Seeing the organization as a means to support the member, the spiritual manager eliminates all but the most necessary structure, seeking to empower each member with all the resources, information, and authority at her command to enable the members to effectively serve the customer's needs.

- **Belief in people.** Basic to everything the spiritual manager does is his deep-rooted trust in the goodness and capability of the organization member with which he works. In the universe we are all united, one body. We may have different roles and talents, but all have equal value.

- **Call to serve.** The spiritual manager sees her vocation as a call to serve other organization members. She realizes the member with which she works produces the goods and services meeting the client's needs, and she sees her job as making sure they have everything they need to get their job done.

- **Provides a safe environment.** Knowing that we all operate in an atmosphere of uncertainty where the best we can do is try to guess what will happen, the spiritual manager is not hung-up on predetermined goals and objectives and creates a place for people to do their best, one day at a time, encouraging an open mind towards any outcome and the lessons it may provide.

- **Challenges and disciplines.** In the spiritual organization, everyone's best effort is vital to seek the accomplishment of the vision. The spiritual manager, in the true sense of being a team, works with his team to help all members succeed. If accomplishing their role in meeting the vision is not possible for a team member, counseling is given to help find the place where his or her talents can best be used, or to help the member move on to more satisfying employment. Although difficult to address, the spiritual manager believes no one benefits from being allowed not to contribute to the vision and, with a caring attitude, takes necessary action.

- **Seeks worthwhile work for self and others.** This time we have been given is time to be well spent and our lessons well learned. The spiritual manager understands the need for meaning in our lives and makes certain all members have work which provides a contribution to the vision and to their own spiritual journey.

- **Seeks to understand, not just to be understood.** The spiritual manager does not try to manipulate members by using their intrinsic motivators to get them to do what he wants them to do. Instead he seeks to truly know the members' dreams and spiritual quest so as to help them accomplish their personal vision as well as that of the organization.

- **Sees all things as precious.** This universe, created by an abundant and loving power, exists for a purpose. The spiritual manager feels a sense of responsibility to be sure that none of this abundance is wasted, her talents, those of other members with which she works, the organization's or the environment's.

- **Seeks inner direction gained through reflection and meditation.** The spiritual manager is fully aware we human beings do not have the answers, nor even all the questions. But we are not alone in this universe, and the spiritual manager recognizes that much direction is available if we seek it and are truly willing to listen.

- **Accepts oneself while seeking improvement.** As a spiritual manager having a human experience, the spiritual manager sees this life and their management role as a learning opportunity. She practices, does some things well, others not so well, but keeps going as she seeks progress, not perfection.

* * *

To summarize, a spiritual style of management is **a consistent way of behaving, based on perceptions of one's self and others as united into one body guided by a universal power, which is aimed at accomplishing organizational objectives.** The spiritual manager operates from a position of wholeness, not "holeness." She sees the universe as one of abundance, supplying all we need as part of creation, not its master.

This completeness within herself helps in dealing with the pressure to try to control others and outcomes so prevalent in past management practices and literature. Let's take an in-depth look at control and what it amounts to in reality.

CHAPTER TWO

Control, The Key Issue:
Who Is Running This Show Anyway?

This chapter does not present solutions. Its purpose is to reinforce the basic premise of the spiritual style of management. We are
not in control. All of our futile efforts to be in control create nothing
but stress in our life and in the lives of others. There are solutions.
We will discuss many of them later but for now we must understand
that we are not running the show. It's my belief that our job is to get
in touch with the natural forces of the universe that are in control
and by going with those forces obtain results far greater than could
have ever been expected given our very limited ability to control the
universe and all its people.

In any organization, in any relationship, control usually becomes
a major issue. The question of who's really calling the shots, who
makes the decisions around here regarding what we do and how we
do it, is present and needs to be addressed. Dominance patterns or
effective ways of controlling other members of the group are present
in many forms of gregarious animal life. Size, force, maturity, ability
to provide, and physical appearance are some of the more obvious
means by which one member of a group seeks to exercise dominance
or control over other members.

There are other less obvious ways we seek control. Always taking
a negative attitude is one. This position, which I call "negative pro-

jecting," gives us a payoff for our pessimism, keeping us hooked by letting us feel we are in control. *Touchstones,* a morning meditation book I read regularly, says it best:

> It creates misery, but serves our demand for control. There is more risk in being open to something positive because we cannot force positive things to occur. We can only be open to them and believe in the possibility. But when we predict the negative and expect only bad things, we squelch many good things or overlook them. Then we say, "I knew it would be this way," and in our misery we satisfy our self-centered craving to be in charge. When we surrender our need to be in control, we are more open and welcoming of the good things that come our way.[1]

One of my sons put it well when he said, "I don't plan ahead, I worry ahead."

*　　　*　　　*

Organizations have traditionally tried to create control through organizational structure, hierarchy, and vesting authority in positions within that hierarchy. Aspiring officers were sent to command and control schools. Business schools preached span of control. Sophisticated management techniques such as management by objectives and performance appraisals through preset, measurable objectives were taught as ways in which managers could maintain control over the organization, its direction, and its employees. Even strategic planning is generally used by top management to control the behavior of the rest of the organization, keeping all concerned in line with pre-determined missions and goals.

We really haven't progressed very far from the baboon pack Desmond Morris described, with its dominant male and well defined and understood pecking order throughout the troop.[2] What is changing is the opportunity for others to become dominant, i.e., females, minorities etc., but the dominant submissive model still holds in most organizations today. Rising to higher organizational levels and becoming increasingly dependent on others to perform, senior management constantly strives to assure effective control over the organization, needing to get the organization to meet management's predetermined goals.

It's no wonder control or dominance or power is so highly sought after in our culture. Based on instinctive drives, faced with a control or be controlled alternative and conditioned by a society that preaches we can be what we determine we will be, many, if not most of us, seek more and different ways to control our environment, others in our lives and ourselves. And, to some extent, even to a large extent for some, it works. I can remember listening to stories of youngsters who created a dream like Conrad Hilton's dream of owning the Empire State Building or Bill Clinton's dream of becoming President of the United States in the image of his hero, John F. Kennedy. The problem lies not in the dream but in the inner feeling of who's responsible for accomplishing the dream. We all know we have got to do the walking if we are going to accomplish the journey. But who provides the map, the tools and resources necessary? Those of us driven by the need to control see it as our responsibility. We have to make it happen or it's never going to get done. We have to stay on top of things. Make sure that everything is falling in place. And trust no one else to make really big decisions.

At the same time I have seen many, many successful people who have accomplished a great deal in their lives without the need to control. They worked hard, yes. They put their entire selves and efforts into the accomplishment of the dream. But there was one significant difference: they knew they were not in control. They saw themselves as instruments through which things were being accomplished and they were open and willing participants in that process. They trusted in some other power — a divine providence, their workforce, or soldiers as in the case of Gen. George S. Patton. In short, they knew they were not running the show but were part of a much bigger picture and were being called upon to do their part in that picture just like everyone else.

In *New Passages,* author Gail Sheehy concludes that preparing ourselves for successful "sageing" and a spiritual path "requires another level of letting go. We need to change the way we measure time and to relax our insistence on control." Even the stage of "Age of Mastery" she describes for an earlier life period could be said to be our attempt to gain control over life leading to the recognition by those older and sager that such control is not possible and that acceptance pays far greater personal dividends.[3]

Otto Rank, quoted in Mathew Fox's penetrating discussion of *The Coming of the Cosmic Christ,* observes "Excessive need to control comes from fear of mortality, trying to control that which cannot be controlled — death. The resurrection is the solution — a spiritual life and belief in our everlasting spirit which transcends this earthly form."[4]

*　　　*　　　*

You see, bottom line, **control is an illusion.** Stop and think about it for a minute. How do you feel when someone is trying to control you, dominate you, manipulate you, to get you to do what it is that they want to have done regardless of what it is that you want? You may, because of the circumstances, comply. But, if you are like me, there is some part of you that does not comply. There is a part of you that holds back, that doesn't fully participate, that will do what's necessary in order to deal with the power that's being exerted upon you. Somehow you will find a way to maintain your own personal integrity when you are being controlled by someone else. The controller may get her way, may get from you the behavior she is seeking. But that behavior isn't all that you are capable of. It is only transitory and temporary, and you will soon revert back to whatever you need to do in order to maintain your own sense of self-worth and self-control. Control is an illusion. Like the mirage in the desert it seems to be there but when you really try to get your hands on it, when you really try to understand what's going on, control doesn't exist.

That's why managers and organizations have spent so much time and so much money and so much effort to try to develop perfect control systems only to have them fail over and over again. Mistakes crop up, failures happen, performances don't come up to predetermined levels. People don't do what they are supposed to do. And it is all the fault of the system because if we just had the perfect system then we would have perfect control. No way! Control is an illusion and to continually seek after it is to expend your talents, time and energy in a fruitless endeavor. Recognize that you are not in control, that you are not running the show and then you can start from a sounder, healthier, stronger base of working with others, all of whom have their own abilities, talents and skills that can be enlisted in the effort — the effort you all seek to accomplish.

*   *   *

Let's take a look at some more scientific approaches to examining our ability to control outcomes in our lives.

As a social and financial planner in the sixties, I was involved in developing many programs: the betterment of life for the elderly, retirement plans and the like. I am pleased to say that many of those plans became a reality, such as Meals on Wheels, Homestead Tax Relief for the Elderly, and the nation's first retirement plan for dairy farmers. But I can also tell you that many of those plans never saw reality. A rule of thumb for a good planner was a plus or minus 20% margin of possible error in a five-year plan. I would suspect that margin of error is even larger in today's turbulent and rapidly changing times. As a corporate planner of the development of new products and new companies, I would be involved in extensive efforts to predict the likelihood of success or failure of these ventures. Teams of highly competent individuals using very sophisticated modeling techniques, with the latest in computer technologies supporting their efforts, would spend months examining and developing models by which we could base our corporate decisions. I would like to tell you that every one of those new products or company acquisitions were 100% successful, but that is not the case. Some worked, some didn't. We simply could not predict with enough certainty all the variables, all the things that might happen between the time of our planning and the time of the actual implementation of the plan. Try as hard as we might, we could not guarantee success in terms of our corporate profitability objectives.

Then as a political scientist, I received substantial training in the utilization of statistical techniques to determine whether or not there was any validity to various hypotheses we would develop regarding why things worked the way they did in our political systems. I can tell you that I developed many a paper where I triumphantly would announce that I could state that variable A caused variable B to occur with a coefficient of determination of .45. Well, how about the remaining .55 statistic that has to do with what causes variable B to occur? That's called the coefficient of nondetermination and generally is disregarded by social scientists in their quest to find something that causes behavior. In other words, most of our theories are based on a less than complete understanding of what really goes on, what really does bring about the results we are looking at. Now don't get me wrong. I am not knocking political science. The application of these statistical techniques gives us considerably more insight as to what does occur, and I am grateful for the training I have received in order to know, understand and utilize these techniques. They are helpful tools but they do not give us the information we need to know what completely controls any behavior. We just don't know. And we can continue to refine and define and break our subjects down into smaller and smaller categories and we will never know completely what causes variable B to occur with complete 100% assurance. There is something still out there unexplainable, unmeasurable. That is a very important part of the picture.

But these are soft sciences. How about the ultimate hard science — physics? Certainly the rigorous application of physics to any question should enable us to predict with certainty what is going to occur. Right? Wrong! Do you want to have fun sometime? Just watch two physicists building different theories, arguing with each other over who is right as to what causes what. In all my years in sales and management I never saw people go at each other as tenaciously or sometimes viciously as two scientists who both believe they are 100% correct in their assumptions.

Speaking of physics, a physicist friend has told me of several theories which have a lot of bearing on this issue of control. One is the idea contained in Heisenberg's work on quantum mechanics. We can never know everything precisely. There is always going to be some degree of uncertainty — especially as we deal with subatomic particles. We can only estimate probabilities of what is likely to happen. In the October 1994 issue of *Scientific American*, Steven Weinberg points out that in trying to establish probabilities of outcomes, the Copenhagen interpretation (of quantum mechanics) holds that measurement of any quantity intervenes in such a way as to cause an unpredictable change in the quantity.[5]

In addition, the theory of chaos basically explains that our attempts to understand and predict the future development of our universe are going to be forever doomed because of the sensitivity of the prediction on knowledge of our present state. Things happen not in an orderly fashion as we might see them but in a chaotic fashion, one which might appear to be random to us because we simply cannot know and understand all the variables involved in determining what brings about a certain action.

*   *   *

Paradoxically, in a world afloat with information, our logical, brain-centered reasoning is falling short. We need to turn to something else to find the direction, to aim these massive information processing machines. That something else is not in the head, but the heart, the gut; it is the hunch, the sudden inspiration, in our intuitive selves where no logic can take us. Naisbitt and Aburdene cite in their 1985 study of new trends that "Intuition and creativity are challenging the 'it's all in the numbers' business school philosophy." They go on to cite well-known business strategist and professor Henry Mintzberg in his finding that the top CEO is a "holistic intuitive thinker who… is constantly relying on hunches to cope with problems far too complex for rational analysis."[6]

Carol Orsborn, co-founder of Orsborn Public Relations Group of Nashville, highlights the importance of spiritual management in her book, *Inner Excellence: Spiritual Principles of Life-Driven Business,* in which she talks about "surrendering control," an idea that is sheer anathema to the traditional mindset. Yet, Orsborn confidently predicts in the book that "the competitive edge in the coming decades will be held by those individuals and companies who can tap into new lifegiving sources of inspiration, creativity, and vitality."[7]

That intuition, hunch, inspiration, or what have you is, I maintain, our contact with some higher power, some force moving the universe who is in control and will show us the way if we will just let it.

From Jung's collective unconscious to Harmon's declaration that the science of Descartes is dead and our inner intuitive selves provide clear understanding and knowledge, scientists and thinkers are

25

recognizing and enunciating the principles of guidance by some higher power, some universal spirit, however we might know it, which can direct our lives.[8] We can tap into that power if we choose.

* * *

Now what does all this have to do with management? The answer is simple: You, your thinking, your planning, your ego, your will are not running the show. All your managing by objectives, performance contracting through goal setting, all your tools and techniques to make sure others do what it is you want them to do are not going to work. They might work in part, you might get a little success here and a little success there. However, you will never fully know or develop yourself and your own potential, nor aid others in developing their potential as long as you try to stay in control. Understand that as long as you try to control outcomes and others, you are dooming yourself to frustration, stress, anxiety, anger, and all the rest of those wonderful fruits of controlling. Letting go of control and using the principles outlined in this book bring about not only personal rewards to you in regards to peace, contentment, and fulfillment, but greater productivity and more benefits for everyone concerned: you, your organization and the others in your organization.

* * *

What this is about is accepting the fact of a power, a force greater than yourself that is directing the universe and you as a part of it. You can choose to fight that power and try to exercise your own will or you can join with the power and let it guide you. You are not in control, but you can **listen to your own inner voice and let that voice direct you.**

I'm not asking you to take a vow of poverty here. Carol Orsborn describes a revelation she experienced while addressing a group of successful business people. She was proclaiming to her audience the values of reorganizing one's life, putting first things first, and that the rewards of life satisfaction would compensate for the reduction of income. Then she realized that just wasn't the case:

> Here I was telling the finest business people in the South that there were more important things than making money, while our bank accounts were reaching all-time highs... we had sliced our hours, suggested to our staff that they cut out overtime; let go of our impressive trappings — and were now more successful than ever![9]

Orsborn concluded that "personal values and quality of life considerations need not conflict with ambition and success. In fact, it is from these very qualities that success will grow." Her audience "had been fully prepared to swallow the concept of downward mobility as a bitter pill of financial punishment with a spiritual reward of incorporating personal values into their lives." Instead, they were exposed to a "stream of consciousness and confessional sounding like ravings of a mad woman." Her conclusion that "you can work less and achieve more" is closely aligned with my own conclusion: You can practice spiritual principles in the work place and achieve more.

Do you want some more examples of how giving up control can pay big dividends to everyone in the organization? Then read *Busi-*

ness Wisdom of the Electronic Elite by Geoffry James.[10] His in-depth analysis of the success of companies led by such modern leaders as Bill Gates, William Campbell, Lewis Platt and others includes many of the key points of this book. Listen to some of the chapter titles: "The Corporation is a Community," "Management is Service," "Employees as Peers," "Motivate with Vision." And those organizations are not doing too bad for themselves and their employee members.

*   *   *

However, many managers find giving up control to be nearly impossible. I know I did. One of the problems is that we are convinced that we know with a high degree of certainty what the outcome should be — so many widgets manufactured or forms processed, or bottom line profits generated, or sales created or whatever. We know what those results should be and we know what should be done to get those results; so we need to control the process. Fact is, we do not know what the outcome should be. We know what we think the outcome should be, but that is not necessarily, in fact it most likely is not, what the outcome should really be. We just don't know. And it is hard to accept that fact.

It is interesting watching experiments with Total Quality Management (TQM). Managers in organizations talking bravely about empowering the worker, delegating authority to the lowest possible level and then using all kinds of devious means to hang on to control. Requiring that workers' process improvement programs be approved before being implemented. Taking back authority delegated, as General Motors seems to be doing now in some of its plants, according to the press. And undermining the process by expecting workers to make improvements while not giving them the authority to change the system.

This isn't an isolated case. There even is literature on sick organizations and one of the key symptoms is the issue of control. Mary Riley, in her thoughtful book *Corporate Healing: Solutions to the Impacts of the Addictive Personality in the Workplace,* identifies addiction to control as one of the process addictions leading to sabotaging the organization to meet one's own sick needs.[11]

*   *   *

Let me give you an example of how control affects others and outcomes. I was fortunate to serve as an advisor in the field of aging to four different national administrations: Presidents Eisenhower, Kennedy, Johnson and Nixon. Four people, all of whom had ascended to the highest elected office in our land but very different people when it came to the issue of control. Let me contrast two of those people. President Kennedy had invited a small group of us to the White House to discuss some of our concerns about the field of aging and what we thought ought to be done at a national level. Standing in the Rose Garden, much like a neighbor's backyard barbecue, watching John-John and Caroline play in the tree house, I found the experience to be exhilarating and exciting. Kennedy was genuinely concerned but knew he didn't have the answers. He asked us questions. He listened carefully. He would make some suggestions for our response and feedback. It was a delightfully open and challenging exchange with an individual who seemed to recognize that he did not have all the answers and knew that he had to involve the people who had at least more answers than he did. The afternoon ended with a tour of the White House Jackie had just remodeled and was without a doubt one of the most memorable events in my lifetime.

Then there was the time I was asked to head up the Social Security Administration in the second term of President Nixon. I was in a good position to do so, serving at that time as president of investment subsidiaries for a major life insurance company, active in insurance industry circles, connected to fellow Wisconsinite Mel Laird who was the President's domestic advisor and known as an individual who had a background both in government and in business. I spent a very informative day in the White House talking to a number of high ranking officials about the position. Finally, when it became apparent that I might be an acceptable candidate for the position, I was told by a very high ranking Nixon administration official the rules of the game: "If we call you up and tell you to fire the best person you've got, you do it — no questions asked." You see, their objective was to get control over the bureaucracy in their second term, and I was going to be put in there to be an instrument of control. Not to really solve problems or to keep Congress happy or serve the American people, but to get control over the bureaucracy. That was Nixon's number one goal. I declined the position, not wanting to place my family or myself in a position with no obvious benefit, with no real opportunity to use my skills and talents to improve this agency which is so vital in the lives of nearly every American.

I don't know if it was because Kennedy's early failure with the Bay of Pigs convinced him that he didn't have all the answers and was truly not in control, or if Nixon's foreign policy successes convinced him that he did have all the answers and was in control, or if it was just the inherent personality of the two men, but I do know that if Kennedy would have asked me to serve I would have been there in a minute, and I would have given everything I had to help his administration be successful.

*   *   *

My personal issue of control became very evident in writing this book. After going through it a number of times, a close friend of mine gave me substantial feedback that basically I was proposing a system of control only instead of the usual techniques of control, I was using the technique of vision or my strategical planning prowess. I still had the answer. I had the vision. And I discerned whether or not people fit in the organization based on their buying into ensuring the vision. My friend pointed out to me that others like Jerry Jones and David Koresh had visions as well. And that what I had in mind could lead to the worst kind of control. I was shocked when he gave me this feedback and, of course, at first denied it. But reading it over through his eyes I could see over and over again how I was still exercising control, in a kinder, softer way perhaps, but still exercising control. It is a tough and continuing issue for me. Even to a point of frustration of deciding that this book was impossible because one cannot move away from control sufficiently and its entire premise is incorrect.

But then I picked up an audiotape of Tom Chappell reading his book *The Soul of a Business: Managing for Profit and the Common Good* and listened to his struggle to fully empower his organization, Tom's

31

of Maine, and I knew I wasn't alone. Despite his best intention, going to Harvard Divinity School, studying for the ministry, and all he accomplished in the world, I could still hear his struggle with control in his voice. But he made wonderful progress in his quest to bring soul into business.[12]

We are not perfect nor do we live in a perfect world. The idea is to make progress. Spiritual progress. And today, with the help of God, my higher power, I will continue to try to be open to making progress and increase my willingness to give up control and turn control of my life and what I accomplish over to Him.

As I began this journey, I realized that the more I know, the more I know I don't know. This necessary and continuing dose of humility moves me from a rigid always-have-to-be-right position to one of being teachable. Then I came to the conclusion that the more I know, and the more I know I don't know, the more I know I don't need to know. An understanding, a certain knowledge, that something out there is guiding my life and I don't need to know what it is or even what I need to do. Then later still, I came to a fuller understanding that the more I know that I don't need to know, the more I know I will know when I do need to know. There is an awareness on my part like the old saying, when the student is ready, the teacher will appear. I believe when I need to know what to do or what direction to take, I will know. It will come to me if I am simply open to the inner messages I receive from my higher power through meditation and through others. It will come to me because I have realized that all I need to know, those vital truths that guide me, I already know but just don't realize them as yet. Those truths are placed in me by the same power that created me, located in my soul, my spiritual link that ties me together with the universe and its creator.

*   *   *

So to answer the question phrased at the beginning of this chapter, who is running this show anyway? The answer is you're not, but it's okay. There is a place for you and a reason for you to be here. It may not be what you thought it was but it is real, it is satisfying, fulfilling, and rewarding. So let go of control. Turn it over to that universal spirit. Be open to what that spirit has for you and you will truly enjoy the fruits of the spiritual style of managing.

You will come to know a deeper and more prevailing peace in your life. You will gain insight into yourself and your behavior that will enable you to look at what you are doing and make necessary changes, enabling you to achieve much higher levels of happiness and satisfaction. And don't discount material success as well. We will cite many leaders and high-level managers who have achieved substantial material success but did so in terms of putting first things first — their relationship to their higher power, a daily active practicing of those beliefs, and a willingness to turn all that material success over to God should it be required. Money and material results are basically surrogates or stand-ins for something else that we want at a deeper level of our life. What a spiritual style of management can provide for you directly are those deeper things that you look for: peace, satisfaction, and meaning. A sense of well-being, of being right with one's self and the world. A sense of fitting in and being whole.

My experience has been that God has always provided for me when I needed his help, including material possessions. I have been

33

able to maintain myself and my family adequately my entire life and have reached a level of income and material wealth I never dreamt possible in my youth. This isn't just my story. It is a story of many others who have shared and have practiced a belief in a spiritual way of living and have practiced that spiritual way of living in their everyday work.

CHAPTER THREE

My Story: Struggling With Control

I see myself as being on a spiritual journey. After several early scrapes with religion, my college years saw a period of atheism, reading books debunking the Bible and God and everything else religious. During the latter part of my college life, my father-in-law introduced me to the Roman Catholic Church. An extraordinarily well-read and faith-driven man, he had a big impact on my life and caused me to begin a rigorous practice of Catholicism which I maintain to this day. Although I have gone through some difficulties in maintaining my active membership, I love my church; nonetheless, this book is not about my church nor is it about Catholicism. It is about a spiritual power in my life that I never came to know through the Catholic Church.

By the time I was in my mid-thirties, I had managed to achieve substantial success. A shoe store manager at age seventeen, I worked my way through college, then entered public service after receiving a bachelors degree in psychology and later a masters in political science/public administration. Following a stint as coordinator of the Lansing, Michigan Project on Aging, I became the first executive director of the Wisconsin State Commission on Aging, serving under three governors and providing leadership to the state in the development of a wide range of programs and services for the elderly. By age thirty-two, my activities resulted in my being named by President

Johnson to the National Advisory Committee on Older Americans, to be named Wisconsin's Outstanding State Employee of the Year, one of Wisconsin's Five Outstanding Young Men, and one of the Outstanding Young Men of America.

From there I left the public sector to enter the world of private enterprise in order to give me the financial resources to eventually run for the U.S. Senate. While the run for the Senate never material-ized, economic success did as I progressed in the insurance and fi-nancial services business to the point of being a member of the se-nior management team of one of America's largest insurance-based financial institutions. It was that company's consulting psychologist who told me, "Jim, you don't have drive; you're driven." To this I replied, "Thanks." You bet I was driven. My life was dedicated to becoming successful, to gathering as much power as possible to en-able me to offset that terrible hole that lay deep inside of me that somehow let me know I was not good enough, that I didn't fit in, that I didn't belong. Somehow I would prove that nagging voice was wrong, that I was good enough, that I could fit in. That I did belong.

When you are raised in a chaotic family unit, as I was, where everything seems to be out of control, the only answer is to try to get control. With a father who was likely to fly off the handle at any minute, and a mother who seemed to be helpless and a victim of the circumstances, life seemed pretty unpredictable. The only thing pre-dictable was I didn't know for sure what was going to happen from one moment to the next. So, there was a real need to have things be predictable. To make things come out the way I expected them to come out—for better or for worse. To do that, I had to have control.

I never knew I was seeking control. I thought I was just doing what a responsible older brother should do, dominate the lives of his younger brothers and sister, take charge of many family affairs and celebrations, make decisions regarding family activities, etc. Dad wasn't there most of the time, Mom needed the help, and so I stepped in and took charge. I don't recall when that first happened, but I know that by the time I was six or seven it was already an ingrained pattern of behavior and one that changed very little the rest of my life. I was responsible. I was in charge. I took control and got things done.

The problem is that when you are in control you have to be right. You can't afford to be wrong. To make a mistake causes everything to fall apart and that tremendous need to be seen as successful goes right down the drain. I remember an important hearing on one of my bills in the Wisconsin legislature, having just finished letting the opponents of this bill know exactly how incompetent they were to judge the real facts of life, when a close associate of mine leaned over and whispered in my ear. "You know, Jim, you're always right." To which I replied, "Thanks." It never occurred to me he was being cynical; I was so convinced I was always right. There wasn't any choice. I had to be right. If I was wrong, things would really be messed up.

My relationship with God evolved pretty much the same way. I was really in charge and running the show, and God was a handy person to take care of little tasks I assigned to him. If we got a problem or if things got pretty tough, I would make a little prayer and say, "God, please take care of this; God, please take care of that; God, please do this." So I made the decisions as to what needed to be done and I just simply enlisted God's help in getting it done. But make no mistake, God was not in charge, I was, or so I thought at the time.

Interestingly, I believe my spiritual journey really took off as a result of a management course. While serving as president of its investment subsidiaries and a member of the Senior Management Team at Unionmutual Life Insurance Company (now UNUM), I was sent to a week-long managerial grid school operated by Scientific Methods. Here I was to become familiar with their process of team management which my boss had decided to implement throughout our organization. Through this training process I began to gain an insight into myself I had never seen before.

My school teammates, who had gotten to know me as well as anybody in my entire lifetime, described my behavior in such terms as "dangerous" and "bulldozer." I was shocked. How could they see me like that? After all, I was the consummate nice guy: diplomatic, tactful, smooth, charming. I used all my guile on my teammates to get them to do what I wanted them to do. And they told me I was a dangerous bulldozer? They were absolutely right. And I didn't like it. I didn't want to be that way.

The realization that I had to begin to change my behavior struck me at a very deep level. But how could I change?

Soon after the managerial grid school, a television program provided me with more direction on my spiritual journey. The program was the musical, *Godspell*. This wonderful tale of the Gospel of St. Matthew relived by Jesus and his disciples in today's Manhattan was a spiritual and life-changing experience for me. I saw Christ as the model of love and the importance of loving one another in the beautiful words of that simple song, *Day by Day*.[1] I wanted so much to be able to love, but I simply did not know how. That behavior had not been particularly well modeled for me in my youth. I really had little understanding of the concept of love.

Only a month or so following *Godspell,* my wife, despite my strong objections, took me to a Worldwide Marriage Encounter (WWME) weekend. Among the many miraculous things that happened in that weekend was that I heard, and was able to comprehend, the simple statement, "Love is a decision."

The next seven years were spent making decisions to love and presenting WWME weekends all over the United States, providing leadership to the movement in different areas. Through WWME I met many spirit-filled priests, sisters, and laypersons who helped me begin to embody a new attitude toward the church, and I started to understand the difference between religion and spirituality.

One of my Marriage Encounter talks was entitled "I Wear the Mask of the Successful Man." It was very important for me to be seen as successful. I would go to any lengths to be seen as successful. If being seen as successful is so important, then you can't take a chance on trusting others to do things right. You have to make sure they do things right. And, of course, right means doing it your way because you have all the answers. This was true for all my relationships, work or home. I had to make sure I could control my wife and children and their behavior because they reflected directly on me and how people saw me. The children I controlled through exercising total authority over them, to the point that they found through running away physically, or through the use of drugs or manipulative behaviors ways to escape my ever-present onerous authority. My wife was another matter. I couldn't use force or authority on her so I used money. I was the sole provider. I kept the money and I doled it out. I had kept control through money.

Work was another matter. My boss told me one day, "Jim, you are a teller and a seller." I didn't realize until years later what he meant. If I were in a position to be an authority over you, I was a teller. Very nicely, for I was a very nice guy, I would "discuss" what I wanted you to do, how to do it, when to get it done by, and expected you to get it done. However, if I worked for you and you were in a position to exercise control over me, I used the skills learned from dealing with my rage-aholic father. By reading people, I could sense what it was they were looking for and by giving it to them, get what I wanted out of the relationship. In either case, I was the one making the decisions, I was the one that needed to get his own way — one way or the other.

Soon after our WWME weekend, my family returned to Madison, Wisconsin where I developed my own insurance-based financial services firm. At this time the family was confronted with some fairly substantial crises. Our children gave us some extraordinary challenges. My business was confronting my style of management. The effects of my desperate attempts to control this sinking ship manifested themselves in an episode of hospitalization due to heart pain.

During this time I was introduced to a support program that would teach me a number of practical spiritual tools to use in dealing with life on a day-to-day basis. However, I soon rejected the program as unneeded. I could do it on my own, or so I thought.

Then my father, who I had detested most of my life as a weak, ineffective failure, became seriously ill with cancer. Fortunately, I had begun to see some of his strengths and had spent a lot of time with him just prior to his illness. After having surgery to remove the cancer, he appeared to be in remission and returned to his home in

Florida. But suddenly the cancer was back and, after a very brief period of hospitalization, he made the decision to terminate all life support systems. Still in Madison when this happened, I realized there was no way to get to Florida in time to see him before he died. So we got on telephone and talked. I told Dad I knew he would soon be with God and asked him to intercede for me with God, to help me with God. His first response was, "Jim, you don't need any help." (He had always seen me as such a strong and successful person.) I assured him that I definitely needed help and he said, "Okay, you got it." And I deeply believe to this day that my father is intervening for me, is assisting me in this spiritual journey.

Having lost and then rebuilt my business, I felt directionless and decided to fulfill one of my goals to retire at fifty. My family and I moved to our condo in Sebring, Florida, selling our home in Madison and making arrangements to turn my business over to long-term, trusted employees.

My retirement lasted about two weeks. A full blown mid-life crisis hit me, rejecting my former life and disparately seeking a new beginning. Consequently, there ensued a divorce and a rapid descent into a pit of life I had never before experienced. Having left behind my possessions to live in a basement of a friend, I found myself overwhelmingly needy, terribly lonely, and wanting so badly to simply die.

So, despite power, money and prestige, reputation, all those things that I had desperately wanted all my life, I was not a happy camper. This way of living didn't work but what would? LETTING GO. Driven literally to the ground and faced with the knowledge that despite everything I could do, I could not control my life and bring about the peace and happiness I sought, I faced a bleak and seemingly hopeless situation. Thoughts of suicide went through my head more than once. I wandered aimlessly through one miserable day after the other, trying to find some way to reorder my life. Gradually, I came to realize I indeed could not manage my own life. But I had seen in others' lives that there might be a greater power who could. To allow that power to run my life I had to let go of control. I had to come to believe that that power was greater than I was, that it cared for me and would not hurt me, and, finally, that I could trust that power to do what was good for me even though I may not judge it was good for me at the time.

I had to understand that I was not God. I was not the center of the universe; I was a small, though essential, part of the universe. I remember standing on the rim of the Grand Canyon one January morning watching a heavy snowfall. I watched all those millions of flakes come down and drift into the huge chasm before me, and as I watched them I realized that I was like one of those snowflakes. Unique and beautiful, yes, but only one of millions and millions of particles that constitute this universe. Yet I realized as I watched those snowflakes drift down into the canyon that I, the snowflake, and millions of others like me created the river and that the river created this magnificent canyon and that if I didn't exist this would be a different universe. While I was not in charge, I definitely had a role to play and contributions to make. My job was not to run the universe but to get in touch with the power that was running it and to do the part that power had set out for me to do. But how to discern what I was to do? That had always been a big question in my life.

I can remember saying if I could only wake up in the morning and God would write in large letters across the sky what he wanted me to do that day, I would be glad to do it. But he never did. So I thought he never sent me any messages. I was wrong. What I came to realize was that God sent me messages all the time. I just didn't like the messages. He was telling me what it was he wanted me to do, but that wasn't the way I wanted to live my life. That's not what I wanted to do. And so I didn't "hear" those messages. Today, I still have to work at listening. It is not one of my greater skills. For me, meditation and time when I simply focus on being quiet, allows me to absorb ideas, inspiration, "intuition" that comes to me from some inner source, gives me all the direction I really need. Others tell me that they get their direction by listening to others. Whether the signals come from inside or outside of us, the true decision is made internally. There is a certainty, a knowing that this is right, this is what I need to hear, this is what I need to do. Then we can go about doing what it is that we feel directed to do.

I had to come to believe that this power, this universal spirit, this God, really did care for me. And would guide and protect me, even through crises. I remember the pain during my mid-life crisis. The hours and hours of misery and loneliness and desperation, the crying, oh God, it was awful. But what I came to see was that it was all for a purpose. It was something that I needed to go through. To be free of what Gail Sheehy in *Passages*[2] calls the guardians of the past enabled me to look at my life in a whole new way.

When I looked at what had been happening in my life in terms of my relationship with God and I realized that the management training programs, *Godspell,* marriage encounter, support programs and all the rest were not just coincidences. I was in the process of learning lessons, that I needed lessons to learn and that there was a defi-

43

nite direction in my life. And so I definitely believed that this God, this power, really did care for me, really would provide for me, if I could only trust him.

That was the final and crucial step. To trust this higher power. To really let go of running everything in my life and to trust that I would be OK. Well, for starters, the way my life was I didn't have too much to lose in trusting that power. Secondly, I came to realize that a lot of my fear came from the higher power I had known in my early life, my father and my transference of that model to God. Getting to know my dad and his many strengths just prior to his death allowed me to understand that God was not my father, but his love and caring for me were as genuine and as real as my father's love and caring for me, even though my father didn't always have appropriate ways to show it.

Trust is not easy. Most of us have sought, thought, done whatever we needed to do to get control over our lives, to bring about certainty, predictability, to help us try to reach some comfort zone where we would feel safe and secure. After years into this journey, I was revisiting my decision to let go of control and I realized I really hadn't. I had made the decision, but as my friend Chief Fox says in his story of the three frogs, making a decision is not what it is all about. Three frogs were sitting on a log and one decided to jump off. "How many frogs are there on the log," Chief Fox would ask me? "Two," I would say. "Wrong," he would say. "There are three. The frog only decided to jump off. He didn't do anything about it." The point is simple, that I had made a decision to let go of control but my behavior, my actions, were still controlling. I didn't like this conclusion. As a matter of fact, I became quite angry as I searched my soul and looked at what I was actually doing. Finally, I just exploded because I knew deep down that my life would not get any better until I let go of trying to predict and control outcomes and took actions that reflected my willingness to let go. If you will forgive the language, I suddenly burst out when talking with a good friend about this part of my life and yelling at God, I said "OK, You son-of-a-bitch, You think You are so damn smart, You take over and run my life. I give up." That really was a decision to let go and to let Him have the control and from that point on my actions began to reflect that decision. Not all at once, I can assure you. It was probably another two years before I made a decision to turn relationships over to God. You see, I was single, needy and desperate, and I really had to have a relationship in my life and so I was still running that part of my life, not very well, I might add. Finally, realizing that mode of control had to go as well, I made a decision to turn my relationships over to God and began to act accordingly.

In spending some time trying to decide what to do with my life, I remembered the days working in academia, the joy of learning, and my desire back then to get a Ph.D. I began a cram course, passing the GRE and gaining admittance to Florida State University's Department of Political Science as a doctoral candidate. Being a part of that department gave me some wonderful opportunities to learn and to share my own experiences through a series of graduate assistantships with the Florida Center for Productivity Improvement, as a research assistant to Dean Charles Cnudde, and finally as a Senior Management Consultant with the Florida Center for Public Management. Following the Ph.D., I decided to stay with the Center as a trainer and teach management seminars to public managers throughout the state of Florida, a job I sincerely enjoy and believe is doing some small good in helping others to get the benefit from their management training, just as I did many years prior at the Managerial Grid School.

The spiritual journey I began long ago is still leading on, and I have no idea where it might take me or what I may do along the path of this mysterious and exciting adventure. My desire is to become closer to the God of my own understanding, God my universal spirit, God my higher power, my supreme energy source. But the results — and credit — will be God's, not mine.

Today I know many things. Who I am and who I am not. I am a spiritual being operating in this physical sphere. I am not God. However, there is an energy surging within me that is linked to my higher power who has given me opportunities to learn many lessons during this lifetime. Hopefully, opportunities to learn will continue, so I may come to know, to love, and to serve God as I understand God.

I came to trust God because I had no choice; life couldn't get any worse. Today, I have choices, many choices as I experience a rich, full, rewarding life. And today, I once again reaffirm my trust in God and willingness to walk in the direction He provides for me. I have let go, at least for today, of trying to control outcomes and concentrate instead on what lies in front of me to do, remembering always to seek His will for me, not the world's will or mine. It really works.

CHAPTER FOUR

Pluses And Minuses Of Control

Wait a minute! Didn't you just get done telling us that control doesn't work? Chapter Two was dedicated to explaining exactly why we are not in control. Something doesn't add up here Jim. Let's look at the record. You have a wall full of plaques citing you for outstanding achievements. You have served at the highest levels of state government, as an advisor to four national administrations, created significant new and meaningful social programs, managed to get people elected to high public positions and, at least according to your wife's divorce attorney, ended up a millionaire with a successful financial planning practice. You say you were a control freak? Well, if that's how control pays off, I am all for it. Forget about this spiritual manager's stuff.

This was the gist of the conversation I had with one of the earlier readers of my book who questioned the validity of my theme against my own experience. It was a wonderful conversation and one that definitely needs to be dealt with in the course of this book.

I used to give a motivational speech called "How Do You Spell Success?" The primary emphasis in that speech was you, how do you spell success. Its main theme was that we have to learn to look inside of us for what we determined to be successful, not what the world tells us or our parents have told us or significant others in our life tell us, but what we determine is success. Those achievements which meet our needs, give us that deep sense of inner satisfaction, a sense of true joy and meaning in life. Many times people would come up to me following the talk literally with tears in their eyes thanking me for helping them to look through the illusion of success and into their own heart as to what they needed to do. I used to tell people who would sponsor me that you had better be prepared for some of your more successful people to change once they start looking inside themselves.

You see, most of my life was spent in an all-out maximum effort to be seen as successful. I have alluded to my background as a wrong side of the tracks kid growing up in a small town where I was put into my proper economic slot. That and many other aspects of my early life created a very strong "I'll show you" attitude. For many years, whether at a conscious or unconscious level I don't know, my primary goal in life was to get enough power and to make enough money so I could go back and buy my hometown and turn it into a garbage dump. I'd show them. My motives were anger, resentment, hurt, and fear. I had that huge hole in my gut and the only way I could fill that hole was to be successful — that is, powerful, wealthy, respected. And the only way I could become successful, the only way I could be sure I would be successful, was to run the show myself. To take over, take charge, take control, take risks, work hard. You want a job done right, do it yourself. The only person you can count on around here is yourself. That's what the psychologist meant when he said I didn't have drive, I was driven.

Now, let's face facts. Driven, controlling people can achieve high levels of success in our economy. For every story I tell about a spiritual manager who has achieved abundance in his life, you can give me examples of dozens of controlling, driven individuals who achieved high levels of success, as our culture defines success — according to materialistic determinations. In the old managerial grid parlance I grew up with, the 9.1 task-driven, controlling manager was known as an individual who could get projects up and get them going, could achieve high levels of success in a relatively short time frame, and was usually thought to be effective in emergency situations. Those are real pluses and real strengths that the controlling manager can bring to an organization. Those are strengths I usually brought. As the first Executive Director of the Wisconsin State Commission on Aging, I organized the agency from the ground up. As the first Director of Experimental Marketing and later first President of its Investment Subsidiaries, I helped take Unionmutual from the sixth oldest insurance company in the United States to a diversified financial services organization. I took a general agency that was in disarray and rebuilt it into a significant and profitable contributor to Unionmutual's field force. These are definite achievements and I, and the others that worked with me to accomplish them, have every right to be proud of them. However, there is another side.

$$* \qquad * \qquad *$$

There are at least three significant shortcomings of the controlling style of managing: 1) While an organization may do quite a bit with a controlling manager, no organization will ever achieve its full potential which is, after all, the full potential of each and every member of that organization; 2) Organizations built by controlling managers do not last; 3) The spiritual, emotional and psychological price we have to pay for that kind of success.

The Failure To Achieve Full Organizational Potential.

I am proud of the things the organizations I have been associated with over the years have accomplished. The thing I wonder is how much more could we have accomplished with a more spiritual based approach? Organizational success in terms of accomplishing a mission is very dependent on the capabilities of the controlling manager. With a very competent, ambitious controlling manager, organizations can accomplish a lot. They do, you see it all the time. Yet no one person can ever match the contributions that the many can make in creating new, innovative, effective ways to fill the organizational mission. The literature is full of examples of how organizations have thrived using new participative, involving, empowering management styles, part of what I call spiritual management. A recent article, "Learning To Harvest Brain Power Gives Companies Competitive Edge" written by Suzanna Barciela of the *Miami Herald,* says, "Knowledge can be a company's greatest asset. But if it is not cultivated, its value depreciates." Citing an Arthur Anderson study from representatives of some of American's finest companies such as Hewlett Packard and Eastman Kodak, she found huge gaps between the recognition that utilization of all knowledge existent in the organization is essential for success and the actual implementation and utilization of that knowledge.[1]

The problem with being a controlling manager is not in getting things done. Controlling managers produce results all the time but not the kind of results necessary to achieve the highest possible excellence of the organization and full potential of all its members.

Organizations Created By Controlling Managers Don't Last

While this may be something of a generalization, it has been very true in my instance. Organizations built with a single, dominant, controlling force, even though they may fare well for a time under the leadership of that force, do not fare well over the long run. Let me give you some personal examples. The project on aging, which was the genesis of ideas like Meals on Wheels, Drop-In Centers for the Elderly, Senior Citizens Day Centers, Senior Citizens Camps etc. and which resulted in being cited numerous times at national levels, went out of existence after my departure to Wisconsin. The Wisconsin State Commission on Aging, which in five years had become one of the most effective small agencies in the United States, able to pass significant legislation and affect major budgetary considerations to benefit the elderly, was downgraded to a bureau in the state welfare agency after I left. Complete Retirement Service, a corporation I created and which provided new and unique services to help employees plan for and benefit from retirement, ceased functioning after I left for Maine. Unionmutual Management Corporation and its subsidiaries, the investment arm of Unionmutual which I led in creating a dynamic, innovative company that was written up in *Money* magazine amongst others, was disbanded soon after my departure from the company. I can remember looking back and thinking that my life was like quicksand. Everything that I created seemed to just disappear. I think I now understand why. Let me relate one short story to explain.

I remember when I started Complete Retirement Service. I needed to bring someone in who could help manage its growth. I was very fortunate in hiring a former vice president of a major Wisconsin bank and a friend of mine from the Jaycees. His first day on the job he drove up in his new Oldsmobile and there on the side of his car was a plastic, magnetized sign proclaiming Complete Retirement Service, our address and phone number. I took one look at that and told him in no uncertain terms that he was to remove that sign. It didn't reflect the image that I had of our company. He got the message: Don't use initiative, don't try to use your brains, wait and see what Jim wants, get your orders and follow them. Later, he went to work as the executive director of one of our largest clients which contributed in part to the downfall of Complete Retirement Service. I don't blame him for what he did, I would have done the same thing. I used to see the same thing in many small corporations where the individual entrepreneur who started the business still had to run every single aspect of that business and was stifling its growth. In the final analysis, business can't grow with that controlling entrepreneur owner who won't let go of the strings. And, likewise, organizations led by controlling managers, no matter how dynamic they may be, do not last beyond that manager.

The Price We Have To Pay

C. S. Lewis, one of my favorite authors, has a quote, "There are only two kinds of people in the end: those who say to God 'Thy will be done,' and those to whom God says, in the end, 'Thy will be done.' All that are in hell, choose it. Without that self choice there could be no hell." Listen to this again..." and those to whom God says, in the end, 'Thy will be done. All that are in hell, choose it."[2]

Driven by that constant need to be seen as successful, beleaguered by a thousand forms of fear, fueled by anger and resentment and hurt, I drove myself and my organizations. All that are in hell choose it. I certainly chose my hell and, unfortunately, inflicted hell on many others, many who were closest to me. I remember belonging to a very highly regarded country club where many of my community's successful business people belonged. I can remember many things from that association; getting to know a lot of successful business people, doing lots of business with them, which was beneficial for myself and my company, enjoying companionship and a sense of belonging. But one thing I don't remember is joy. Our bar tabs, condos, automobiles, boats and other playthings gave eloquent testimony to our constant effort to find joy somehow in this materialistic, success-driven world we lived in. I can't speak for others there, but I know there was no joy for me in that success-driven, controlling, competitive environment. That's an awful price to pay.

One of my meditational readings suggests:

> If we take time to watch animals, we see that they
> have a zest for life that seems to engage them totally
> in whatever they are doing. A cat chasing its tail, a
> dog going after a ball, a horse running along the shore,
> a dolphin leaping and diving. All are actions that re-
> veal energy and delight in simply being alive.
> Life we say is to be enjoyed but how many of us man-
> age to put this theory into practice?... If we can tap
> into the spontaneity that runs through the animal king-
> dom, we will rediscover the sheer joy of being alive.[3]

There was no sheer joy for me in this controlling, success-driven lifestyle I was living.

Another of my readings quotes Arthur Jersild in discussing compassion. "It is through compassion that a person achieves the highest peak and deepest reach in his or her search for self fulfillment." To be compassionate is to go "outside our own self-centered egos and care about someone beyond ourselves. In the process we are helped and changed — perhaps more than the person we are helping."[4] It is so hard to be truly compassionate and caring for others, as I believe we are called to do, when we simply see them as a means to fulfill our driven need to be successful, to achieve, to control. They are not persons to love, they are objects to get to do what it is that we want them to do so we can get our needs met. That's an awful price to pay in relationships.

*   *   *

Even as my readings highlighted the price I paid as a controlling manager, so, too, did others give me solutions. One is from the *Manual for Teachers - A Course to Miracles.* In answering the question "How should the teacher spend his day?", they answer,

> To the advanced teacher of God, this question is meaningless. There is no program for the lessons change each day. Yet the teacher of God is sure of but one thing; they do not change at random. Seeing this and understanding that it is true, he rests content. He will be told all that his role should be, this day and every day.[5]

As a spiritual manager, like an advanced teacher of God, I need not worry about what I should do today. I am not in control and I

54

will be told what I should do this day and every day if I will but listen. I can give up control and know joy and have compassion and have an abundant life.

In the *Seven Spiritual Laws of Success,* Deepak Chopra cites his fourth spiritual law of success, the law of least effort. He says:

> When you remain open to all points of view — not rigidly attached to only one — your dreams and desires will flow with nature's desires. Then you can release your intentions, without attachment, and just wait for the appropriate season for your desires to blossom into reality. You can be sure that when the season is right, your desires will manifest. This is the law of least effort.[6]

I do not need to make people, places, and things conform to my will. I need to be open, not only to God's Will for me but to others as well. And in the spontaneous sifting through, come to a common understanding which provides us all with direction and achievement in a true sense of spiritual community which will know abundance. Even as we make our own hell, we can make our own heaven. Even here, on earth, even here at work. Let me give you one final example from my own life. After having begun this spiritual journey as a result of my attendance at the Managerial Grid School, marriage encounter and other experiences, I returned to Madison, Wisconsin to rebuild an insurance agency and to provide financially for my family. But something had changed. The need to control had begun to disappear and my focus was much more on what it was we were trying to accomplish, and in enlisting and empowering people to truly help accomplish that mission. And I had people with amazing strengths willing to contribute above and beyond the call of duty to make the organization successful. Together we built the organization, and even though we came upon hard times with the termination of our Unionmutual General Agency contract, we were able to continue to regroup and to grow again. Then came my mid-life crisis and my inability to maintain any kind of meaningful role in that business. Yet the business continued and continues to this day under the leadership of a former agent and my staff.

Today, God continues to provide and I still have relatively little to do with it. Opportunities come up, things appear for me to do and I get paid for doing them. I am not in control today. I am not running the show. And it is very clear to me who is. I am not on welfare; I have a very nice lifestyle. The anger, hatred, resentments and fears of the past are gone. I went back to my fortieth class reunion after having let everyone know of all my accomplishments, my Ph.D. etc. (after all, I am still human). I saw my classmates for what they were — nice people doing what they did then and doing what they do now, because that's what they do. They are not doing it at me or to hurt me as I thought for so many years.

Having to have control may have paid off in the short term, but not when or where it counts. I do not want to have control any more and I am not willing to pay the price it requires. Turning my will and my life over to the care of God works far better for me and, I think, for those around me.

*   *   *

Yet even as I give up control and focus on the things to do today, I still need a dream, a vision of where I am going, of my destination. The difference is I no longer create that vision. Today I simply seek to know a higher power, to be open to his vision for me, to have others share their visions and together form a visionary community, relying on God's power to help us make the dream a reality.

CHAPTER FIVE

Vision, The Key For Unity:
Running In The Same Direction

All right, we're not in control, despite what the organizational chart says. Still, we're held accountable for results and as managers our job is to get results with and through other people. So how do we do that, if we are not running the show?

We don't need to run things if everybody is running in the same direction. The question is how to have everyone in the organization going the same way. Effective managers have found that is best done by having a shared vision for the organization with everyone involved in producing the results.

The literature is full of vision, the need for vision in organizations, leaders have to be people of vision, etc., but I don't think anyone has captured vision, at least from my perspective, as well as Emmanuel. Listen to what he says:

> You need to know the great power that lies
> in the act of visualization.
> Vision is spiritual reality, and all things
> that exist in your world first existed in spirit.
> The concept comes first, then the physical,
> which is denser matter, follows.
> Once you challenge your preconceptions,
> they become misconceptions.

The diameters of your awareness expand.

A wall, for instance, is no longer only a wall

but a bit of moving, vibrating consciousness.

Anything that can be envisioned

can be brought into your physical reality.[1]

There is great power in the act of visualization. Not just your vision, but our vision.

By sharing the vision and mission, everyone sees a common reason for the existence, calling, and purpose of the business. We align with others who understand and feel the same as we do concerning the direction we are taking, what we want to accomplish, how our work serves our higher power, others, and ourselves. **Our vision provides the direction we all need and with that shared vision there is no need for me to try to control others or outcomes.**

You see, having no idea as to what God's plan really is for me and for this universe, I have to be open to almost anything that comes to me in terms of that inner inspiration or intuition. I have found that it is not necessarily "holy" stuff that comes to me, but lots of things like types of bonds to invest in, improvements needed in social services, better ways of moving goods and services etc. The ideas, inspirations and intuitive insights that come to help form your vision seem to be almost endless.

Sharing The Vision

Like a lot of management terms today, vision is overused and abused. Let's make sure we are communicating what we mean by vision.

First of all, what we do not mean is something somebody in the "head shed" cooks up to get the troops all doing what it has been decided needs to be done. This "creating" the vision and "selling" the vision is not what we are about. Nor is vision about the purpose of the business, its reason for existence. In my parlance that's the mission of the organization. Mission is the unifying force that brings everybody together in agreement as to why we are here. Everyone should have input into the development of the mission but the mission, after all, is the core of the business or the organization. It should be understood, agreed and committed to by all members of the organization, and they should clearly understand their role in fulfilling the mission of the organization and their importance to it. But that is not the vision.

Our vision is our shared dream. It's what we want to accomplish. The benefits that we want to provide. The people we want to serve and the way we want to serve them. Visions are images we carry in our heads that we constantly hold before us as those ideals we seek to make reality.

In *The Fifth Discipline - Building Shared Vision,* Senge stresses,

> If any one idea about leadership has inspired organizations for thousands of years it's the capacity to hold a shared vision of the future we seek to create. One is hard pressed to think of any organization that has sustained some measure of greatness in the absence of goals, values and missions that become deeply shared throughout the organization. IBM had "service"; Polaroid had instant photography; Ford had public transportation for the masses and Apple had computing power for the masses. Though radically different

in content and time, all these organizations managed to bind people together around a common identity in a sense of destiny.

When there is a genuine vision (as opposed to the all too familiar "vision statement"), people excel and learn not because they are told to but because they want to… What has been lacking is a discipline for translating individual vision into shared vision — not a "cookbook" but a set of principles in guiding practices.

The practice of shared vision involves the skills of unearthing shared "pictures of the future" that fostered genuine commitment and enrollment rather than compliance. In mastering this discipline, leaders learn the counter-productiveness of trying to dictate a vision no matter how heartfelt.

I strongly urge you to read his chapter on vision but just a few more quotes:

A shared vision is not an idea. It is not even an important idea such as freedom. It is, rather, a force in people's hearts. A force of impressive power. It may be inspired by an idea but once it goes further—if it is compelling enough to acquire the support of more than one person—then it is no longer an abstraction. It is palpable. People begin to see it as if it exists. Few if any forces in human affairs are as powerful as shared vision.

Like myself, Peter Senge cautions against the use of vision as a method of management to manipulate the people in the organization. He points out that "such visions at best command compliance — not commitment. A shared vision is a vision that many people are truly committed to because it reflects their own personal vision."

Senge goes on to describe how you can work through the process of enrollment and commitment to shared visions.[2]

Naisbitt and Aburdene, in *Reinventing the Corporation,* highlighted the role of vision as a key component in the reinventing process. "We believe the first ingredient in reinventing the corporation is a powerful vision — a whole new sense of where a company is going and how to get there..." While they fall into the trap of a top-down visioning process, the authors do point out that "the idea is simply that by envisioning the future you want, you can more easily achieve your goal. Vision is the length between dream and action." They also go on to point out the use of vision and visualization in athletics today.[3]

It reminded me of the session I attended on learning how to putt more proficiently. As a somewhat high-handicapped golfer I had the usual desire to improve my putting, and a friend of mine, a sports psychologist at Florida State University, was putting on a seminar for local golfers on use of imagery in improving their putting process. She kindly invited me to attend the seminar and it was an extremely interesting experience. First, she put us through a series of relaxation exercises to be able to relax our body and our minds to create a more receptive environment. Then, a film was played showing the putting stroke from every conceivable angle — on top, by the side, over and over and over again. And over and over and over again I saw that stroke. I could literally begin to feel that stroke. Elbows out, wrists firm, head down, stroke the ball. And to see that ball literally fall into the hole. Years later, I can still see that image. I can still feel that stroke and see that ball dropping in the hole.

The use of vision and visioning is extremely powerful if it is truly a shared vision, not one imposed on people, but one that people come to see, understand and commit to of their own volition. One that they want in their lives as much as you want in yours.

One of the earlier authors that touched on visioning and visions was Henry Thoreau in *Walden: Or Life in the Woods*. Listen to what he had to say:

> I learned this at least by my experiment. If one advances confidently in the direction of his dreams and endeavors to live the life which he has imagined, he will meet with a success unexpected in common hours. He put some things behind, will pass an invisible boundary; new universal and more liberal laws will begin to establish themselves around and within him; or the old laws be expanded and interrupted in his favor in a more liberal sense and he will live with a license of a higher order of beings.[4]

*   *   *

Living The Vision

No matter how many times I see the ball falling in the cup, I still have to putt it to make it happen. Visions are powerful, absolutely necessary to pull us together, give us common direction and commitment to each other. However, as managers there are some specific things we need to do in order to fully utilize the vision in order to obtain results for which we are held accountable. They are selection, orientation, supervision and termination. Let's look at each.

Selection

In terms of selecting new members, once basic technical competencies are established and the quality of the character is determined, the main item for screening and selecting potential members of your employment community is their understanding and commitment to the organization's mission. The organization's vision shared by existing members must be thoroughly developed for the prospective member. Complete honesty must be encouraged in what is involved to move toward the vision, both on your part and on theirs. Even though new, they might have thoughts or concerns about the mission and vision which should be fully explored. Both parties need to have all the facts necessary in making a decision whether or not to form a relationship. The use of mission and vision and full involvement of fellow members in the selection process will greatly facilitate the development of a vision community.

Orientation

Once on board, new members need thorough orientation and training to help them develop the skills and knowledge necessary in order to accomplish their essential role in the vision community. Most of the orientation will be done by fellow workers in the community. It is they who welcome the members, bring them in, answer the questions, support them, encourage them and help them develop their understanding of the vision and their role in the workplace. During the period of technical training some relatively close assistance may be necessary to help them develop the skills to accomplish their tasks. This can be done either by management, an outside training facility or in most cases by the co-workers themselves. The concept of a lead worker who enjoys the responsibility of assisting new people in developing their skills might be a key role in your community. Also, be aware of the fact that if the community does not truly share the vision, it will soon become apparent to the new member and will result in lack of trust, reduced morale and productivity. You must be prepared to fully live the vision, mission and values you espouse or else do not espouse them.

Supervision

We have long known that achievers want information, want to have a say in what it is that they do and want recognition for having done it. All efforts should be focused on accomplishing at least some small part of the vision in any given time frame. These objectives should not be set by someone and put down on the worker. They should be mutually discussed by the manager and the member, and the member should decide what can be accomplished in this time frame and what will be required in order for them to accomplish it. The manager's role will be to assist members in getting the tools, resources and authority necessary to accomplish the objectives they have laid out for themselves in accordance with the vision they share for their unit.

Termination

It is a fact of life that not everyone will, despite all of our efforts, fit into the vision community. Personal problems which detract from their ability and which are beyond the scope of the workplace, basic lack of skills and abilities, and severe attitudinal problems can occur, and our best efforts of working with, coaching and helping the employee do not bring about the results necessary to accomplish our shared vision. Others may have verbalized support for the shared vision in order to obtain employment but really don't agree with it and they operate on values inconsistent with those of the community. Here it may become necessary to separate the individual from the community through termination of employment. This is not an easy task but a necessary one. In discussing this, I was particularly disturbed by my friend's input that basically I was saying it's my way or the highway. Buy into my vision or you are out the door. Just a modern version of top-down hierarchial management. Knowing my tendency for controlling in my management roots, I could readily see the validity of his input. I began a fairly extensive search of literature to see if I could find some answers to how to handle this difficult problem. One of the sources I turned to was a book entitled *Business By The Book, The Complete Guide of Biblical Principles for Business Men and Women* by Larry Burkett. In developing the biblical principles for firing, Burkett outlines some very clear and standard approaches to termination which come right out of standard management texts such as clearly defined job descriptions, job standards, full communication of expectations, concern for job performance, a trial correction period and then dismissal.

One thing he cautioned against was reacting against the "heavenly sandpaper" factor. Someone might just be a real burr under your saddle and challenging you and the vision but they are really helping you and your organization's development as a community. He says,

"I don't know if God has ever used someone as 'heavenly sandpaper' in your life, but he most certainly has in mine. If you recognize this, don't dismiss that person. If you do, God will simply bring another just like him into your life to polish off those rough places."[5]

Another source I turned to was the *Tao On Management,* a tape by Bob Messing and Ken Blanchard. There I found the Tao to speak in military parlance; when faced with an employee who appears not to be helping the community in the fulfillment of its vision, several steps were outlined: 1) be careful to not take any rash action which might result in casualties which would be harmful to the organization at a later time; 2) consider the possibility of a retreat, it may be better to give in a little than to take action which could be harmful to the organization; and 3) if necessary, managers should be prepared to take action to terminate the employee after having considered all the factors above. The Tao advises that in such times it is necessary to punish those who do damage to the organization and to reward those who support it. But the Tao stresses in times of peace, militancy is not necessary; the general should retire.[6] This says to me that in ordinary times these actions should not be necessary and should be called upon only if absolutely necessary to preserve the integrity of the vision community.

A way to assist this process would be to encourage the nonperforming employee to engage in a "360 degree" appraisal of his performance. He should seek input from all sources — fellow workers, the manager, any individuals he might happen to supervise, peers in his profession, customers he may serve or vendors with which he may deal. Using this input, he may then perhaps look at his own performance and be able to either correct this performance or if not able to do so, bring about his termination, especially if help can be given to him in separating from the organization and finding new employment.

*   *   *

<u>The vision is not a statement.</u> It is a living, breathing process that is in the mind and heart of every member of the working community that constantly serves as a guide to direct their actions, their decisions and their results and which well may change over time as the community and the world it serves evolves.

Explaining, listening, sharing what we each have learned about the vision and what we need to do today to make it a reality is the core of our management practice. Those who share our vision do not need to be controlled. They have the same built-in controls we have: a desire, a dream, an urge to accomplish the same thing, to go in the same direction, to realize the same vision. Remember Peters and Waterman's great book *In Search of Excellence*[7] and their discussion of simultaneous loose-tight properties? Here they discussed the legends of prominent and successful business leaders who had strong beliefs, strong values, which they rigorously adhered to and built an organization around while at the same time giving members of the organization plenty of rope to be able to operate freely as long as they were consistent with and true to those values. That's what I am talking about. Selecting and working with others who share or will come to share the vision and agree on the results necessary to bring about its accomplishment. Then let them and their higher power operate freely in accomplishing that vision.

As managers and leaders our task is to be open to the vision, to help focus and enunciate that vision so that others who share it can join with us and accomplish a common goal. I have found for myself that it is necessary for me to write down my vision, to listen to others and be willing to clarify that vision so that all have the same understanding of it and then to constantly keep it in front of me as the guiding light of all my behavior. Unless I do this, my human nature will cause me to wander off in different directions. If I do that, or if others in the organization do that, then we lose our effectiveness. We are not working together and differences and dissension can be the result. I need not enforce that vision. Those of us that share it together enforce each other in our joint efforts to accomplish the vision. I need to be as open to others in the organization as I would want them to be to me in terms of taking input from them as to how they see my behavior and its consistency with our shared goals and vision. If they see me doing things differently than what we have all agreed we want to do, they need to tell me about it, and I would want them to.

Obviously, a vision isn't everything. Ford's vision was obscured by a management so obsessed with control they destroyed the founder's vision of the workplace which led to bloody labor wars as workers sought to protect their human rights.

So we need to continue to examine management practices, those processes necessary to create a truly spiritual style of management, ingredients such as the organization itself.

CHAPTER SIX

Organizational Simplicity: The Span Of Uncontrol

Business students are familiar with the famous span of control concept developed by Max Weber and his study of the late 19th century German army. How many soldiers can an officer command in order to make sure that the soldier carries out orders and does what he is supposed to do? Today's modern bureaucracy, public or private, built on the same premise usually has layer upon layer upon layer of management whose basic responsibilities are to make sure that someone from above's orders are carried out. Textbooks tell us this works fine if you want uniform output requiring rigid adherence to standards leading to control over every aspect of the organization. Experience tells us it doesn't work. Results are not uniform. After trying every trick in the book, you have to realize top-down management doesn't give you control. Look at the results of your efforts to control. What do you really get out of all that work? Actually, top-down management is not only useless, it is negative and wasteful once you realize you don't have control and that the real power in the organization lies in a group of individuals who share a common vision and who utilize their talents and skills in order to accomplish that vision.

The only reason to have an organization is to facilitate the ability of the worker, the individual actually producing goods and services, to satisfy the mission of the organization in meeting the needs of its customer. Anything else that's done in any organization is a waste of time and effort, and produces negative results rather than positive. For example, chief executive officers should always remember that one of their primary functions is to create an organization able to get the resources, whether it be in terms of investment capital or budgetary allocations in a public agency, to ensure that the employee has the tools, training and material necessary to provide the goods and services to the customer.

Obviously, the organization guided by spiritual concepts is going to look radically different than that guided by Weber's span of control concept. For instance, Stephen Covey talks about the key issue of trust in his alignment at the organizational level. He asks:

> What would your organization look like in a low trust culture with a control style of management? Very hierarchical. What is the span of control? Very small. Because you can only control so many people. You result to "gofer" delegation; you prescribe and manage methods. Your information system gathers immediate information on results so you can take decisive, corrective actions. You use the carrot and stick motivation system. Such primitive systems may enable you to survive against soft competition but you are easy prey for tough competitors...
>
> If you have high trust, how is your organization structured? Very flat, extremely flexible. What is the span of control? Extremely large. Why? People are supervising themselves. They are doing their jobs cheerfully without being reminded because you have built an emotional bank account with them. You have com-

mitment and they are empowered. Why? Because you have built a culture around a common vision on the basis of certain bedrock principles and you are striving constantly to align strategy, style, structure and systems with your professed mission... and with the realities out there in the environment...[1]

Another case in point is the example that Tom Peters cited in his book, *The Tom Peters Seminar — Crazy Times Call for Crazy Organizations*. He talks about Octacon, a hearing aid manufacturer, which was in trouble. Their president, Lars Kolind, did not reorganize, he disorganized. He changed the company into what he called "a spaghetti organization," a concept without a center. You can read about it in Peters' book but what was interesting to me was what Kolind, who attributed the tremendous rebound and success of his organization to the new structure, said, "We have a tremendous competitive advantage because we don't care about formalities. We only care about performance and results."[2]

*   *   *

Looking at the organization in this light, one could ask, do we need management at all? My answer is yes, definitely. Maybe not as many managers, but effective facilitators, those who truly enjoy working with and aiding others, are essential to the modern organization. But the role of the spiritual manager is much different than the role of the controlling manager. The tasks are those of focusing and enunciating the vision and helping others develop their skills and abilities so they can be maximized in its accomplishment. Yes, managers are needed but they are not needed to control the troops. They are needed to inspire, to lead, to work with others so that the whole organization can accomplish its purposes and meet the goals jointly set by its members.

So then, how many "subordinates" should a spiritual manager be able to work with on an ongoing basis? Isn't subordinates a terrible word? Sort of like subhuman or subpar. It ought to be abolished as a management idiom. I prefer "members" and will generally use that term throughout. The Japanese systems and others which recognize the value and ability of the individual members have focused on a ratio of 30 employees to every manager. That's definitely progress away from the kind of controlling one-to-six ratios we commonly see in traditional organizations, but is it enough? Emerging new organizations today are looking at ratios of up to 100 workers per manager, especially in small entrepreneurial type organizations incorporating the spiritual style. The question is not how many employees per manager on some fixed ratio basis, but the mission of the organization, the shared vision, the complexity of the task, the need of others to receive support, training, and encouragement in meeting the demands of that task. That will give you some idea of the span of uncontrol that may be appropriate for you and your organization.

We need to be clear that we are talking about true managers here. So many of my manager students are truly not managers. They are sort of lead workers who have responsibility for doing lots of things and sort of incidentally "manage" one to six people on sort of a part-time basis. Most of these people really are not managers. They are doers. They are people who have responsibility and a preference for doing things, carrying out the tasks themselves and incidentally directing the work of others. In the spiritual organization these people are not managers. They can very well fulfill the role of lead worker where they can assist some of their fellow members in learning the tasks or dealing with some complex problems from time to time but they are not truly managers. When we speak of a manager/member ratio, we are talking about an individual whose sole concern is the full and complete development of each individual in that unit and the unit itself in order to achieve its full potential, in fulfilling its mission and working towards its vision for the future.

*   *   *

How does this work in a huge organization with thousands and perhaps hundreds of thousands of employees?

One answer seen more and more frequently today is that there is no such thing as an organization with thousands or hundreds of thousands of employees. They may all belong to some common corporate or agency structure but they do not constitute an organization. An organization can be up to 300 individuals working in a vision-driven unit where they share common goals, support each other, and derive common satisfaction from the accomplishment of those goals. The manager is the spiritual leader of that unit who facilitates the development, understanding and commitment to the shared vision and helps all members use their skills and talents to meet that vision. Others participate in that task by training each other, supporting each other, encouraging each other, helping each other stay focused on the vision. The manager member facilitates the process and provides the leadership through his or her own behavior to encourage others.

An example of this type of leadership comes from rapidly growing Boston Chicken, now known as Boston Market, a family food restaurant chain. In the article "Lessons from America's Fastest Growing Companies" in *Fortune Magazine,* Boston Chicken was prominently mentioned as an outstanding example and ranked high in the Top 100 fastest growing companies in America. Listen to what they have to say about structure. These executives (CEO Scott Beck, Vice Chairman Saad Nadhir and Jeffrey Shearer) are constructing a flat anti-hierarchical company based on the power of information. "We wanted to create a business where managers at the operating level have the expertise and knowledge to drive the company forward themselves," says Beck. "We at the corporate level would just be facilitators."[3]

To see if this was just rhetoric or fact, I recently talked to a local "proprietor" in Tampa, Florida. When asked if there were any substance to this statement, she said, "absolutely." "This is my store and I have the responsibility and the authority to make sure it works." When I asked her if that was true only for her, she assured me it was not. "Any member of our crew has the authority to do whatever it takes to serve our customers," she said. Words I have heard from other excellent providers such as the Ritz-Carlton hotel chain.

*   *   *

Unit tasks may be broken down into smaller units where members of that unit particularly focus on their portion of the vision. All members are responsible for maintaining data and information to help them manage their units.

One example of this approach to organization was the Wal Mart

Corporation. Sam Walton, in his book *Made in America,* shares lots of his own philosophy about the organization. Interestingly, in reading the book it occurred to me that Sam might have been sort of a control freak. When asked how many stores he thought he could possibly develop, he opined that maybe he could get up to nine variety stores because it would be "unwieldy" to manage any more stores by himself. Something obviously happened as Walton relates the tremendous growth of his organization from that first store in Newport, Arkansas to becoming the largest retailer in the world. He comes to this conclusion:

> Here's the point; the bigger Wal Mart gets, the more essential it is that we think small. Because that is exactly how we have become a huge corporation — by not acting like one. Above all, we are small town merchants and I can't tell you how important it is for us to remember — when we puff up our chests and brag about all those huge sales and profits — that they are all made one day at a time, one store at a time, mostly by the hard work, good attitude and teamwork of all those hourly associates and their store managers, as well as by all those folks in the distribution centers.

You see, he saw the value and ability of all members to carry out the vision. He goes on to say:

> If we ever get carried away with how important we are because we are a great big $50 billion chain — instead of one store in Blythville, Arkansas or McComb, Mississippi or Oakridge... or ever forget that looking a customer in the eye and greeting him

or her and asking politely if we can be of help is just
as important in every Wal Mart today as it was in that
little Ben Franklin in Newport — then we ought to
go into a different business because we will never survive in this one.[4]

Walton outlines his six ways in which Wal Mart tries to think small.
That and the rest of the material he shares is well worth reading.

* * *

Another approach to breaking up the organization is outlined by
Tom Peters in his book *Liberation Management.* Citing Quinn Mills in
his *Rebirth of the Corporation,* Peters discusses clusters as an alternative to hierarchy. "These largely self-sufficient clusters vary in size
from 30 to 50 people as Mills sees it and are further divided into self-
directed work teams of five to seven people each...." A cluster is defined by Mills as:

> ... a group of people drawn from different disciplines
> who work together on a semi-permanent basis. A clus-
> ter... handles many administrative functions thereby
> divorcing itself from an extensive managerial hierar-
> chy. A cluster develops its own expertise, expresses a
> strong customer-orientation, pushes decision making
> toward the point of action, shares information broadly,
> and accepts accountability for... results.

Peters then goes on to discuss the case history of Johnsonville
Foods of Johnsonville, Wisconsin. Having spent part of my growing
up years in Sheboygan and Sheboygan Falls, and being a big fan of

one of Johnsonville's products, the bratwurst, I read this with a great deal of interest. Peters relates that Ralph Stayer, upon assuming leadership of the organization in 1978, realized that his top-down management style was having a direct impact on the employees. Stayer recalled an incident in 1980 that made a big impression. "I hired one employee early on who was very competent," Stayer said. "Then one day it struck me that he was just a soldier carrying out my orders. I tried to get him to take on more responsibility but he couldn't. I had ruined him! A few years of my style had beaten the independence out of him." Stayer goes on to say, "It wasn't because our employees were bad people," he added. "If anything needed fixing, it was me."

Peters describes the functions of a typical dozen-person Johnsonville work group, whose responsibilities include recruiting, hiring, evaluating and firing their members on their own, acquiring new skills and training one another, developing and amending their own budget, making capital investment proposals, handling quality control, constantly improving every process and product, developing quantitative standards for productivity and quality and monitoring them, suggesting and developing prototypes for possible new products, fully integrating their counterparts from sales, marketing and product development (if a customer has an idea or a complaint they talk to the sausage maker not the sales person) and participating in corporate-level strategic projects. What's the impact of all this? Well, Stayer says,

> First of all, you are going to get hired by your fellow
> workers… second you are going to get trained by your
> fellow workers, the people who do the work on the
> job. Third, they are going to tell you how your perfor-

mance stacks up… Your fellow workers are going to
let you know what the performance standards are and
they are awfully high here.

How does this form of management work where basically "management" has gotten out of the way and let the workers run the business? "Johnsonville has grown from around $7 million of revenue in
1981 to about $130 million in 1991." Even more interesting are some
of these quotes from people who work there.

Plant Manager: We are teachers. We help people grow.
That's my main goal. Each person is his or her own
manager. I was involved as a coach. We have people
in the plant who are looking at it and saying, you
know, if we did it this way, if we put in this little piece,
we could take this person out of there and we could
run another 40 pounds. These people are industrial
engineers… businessmen… economists. They own
and operate their own business. Each person at
Johnsonville can do the same thing.[5]

You can read more about Johnsonville foods in Stayer and Belasco's
new book, *The Flight of the Buffalo.*[6]

In *Power Shift,* Ivan Toffler spends a considerable amount of time
looking at what's happening with power and the shift of power in
organizations. This renowned futurist sees "the spread of the profit
center," which has seen many once monolithic companies broken
into semi-autonomous, independently accounted units each responsible for its own operations and its own profit and loss. Toffler sees
this as only a first step "toward the eventual dissolution of the company altogether, automized into a network or consortium of com-

pletely independent contractors or free entrepreneurs. In this model every worker is free-lance, contracting with other free-lancers to get specific jobs done." He goes on to say, however, "The day of total individualization of work, the ultimate dream of the theologically committed free marketeer is far distant. Instead, we can expect profit centers to become smaller and more diverse without disappearing into millions of one-person firms." He proposes the concept of the flex firm. "The flex firm is a broader concept which implies an organization capable of encompassing both the formal and informal, the bureaucratic and the network suborganizations. It implies even greater diversity." He believes that to blindly use some of the "new" organizational principles such as the network structure is to "imply much the same uniformity that bureaucracy imposed albeit at a higher, looser level." But inherent in "the emerging flex firm of the future… are basic changes in the power relationships of employees and their bosses… Power is shifting on the shop floor as well as in the executive suite." In discussing the emergence of the autonomous employee, Toffler cites a GE plant in Salisbury, North Carolina where machine operators have authority to make decisions, take responsibility for repairs, order parts, do whatever is necessary in order to accomplish their tasks. How does it work? "Together they have cut worker hours per unit of production by two-thirds and have slashed the time to customer delivery by 90 percent."

Toffler does an excellent job of following the development of our workforce policies from the agrarian culture to the industrial revolution to what he calls today's "electronic proletariat." He concludes by saying:

It is one of the grand ironies of history that a new

kind of autonomous employee is emerging who in fact does own the means of production. The new means of production, however, are not to be found in the artisan's toolbox or in the massive machinery of the smokestack age. They are instead crackling inside the employee's cranium — where society will find the single most important source of future wealth and power.[7]

While those in the public sector may not have progressed as far as some in the private sector in simplifying their structure, Osborne & Gaebler in their trendsetting book, *Reinventing Government,* highlight some outstanding examples. Their findings, mission driven public organizations "turn their employees free to pursue the organization's mission..." and after eliminating layers of management, teams seem to naturally evolve. These public "task-oriented organizations do whatever it takes to produce results... they typically change their structure and procedures as their tasks change." They are "in effect a continuously variable organization structure," according to social psychologist Roger Harrison.[8]

*   *   *

Freed of being a message carrier between higher levels of management and its employees, freed of the constraints of policy-based, rule-driven organizations, yet thoroughly committed to the mission of the organization and understanding the obligation of returning an investment to the stockholder or to the taxpayer in terms of profits or outstanding service, the spiritual manager can devote his or her efforts to serving the members who are ultimately responsible for producing the goods and services to fulfill the mission of the organization.

Interestingly, Sam Walton's concern about getting big might be justified as I watch the performance of Wal Mart's management since his death. Sam said that he worried about thinking big all the time. He said, "If anybody at Wal Mart thinks we as a company are immune to 'Big Disease,' I wish they would just pack up and leave right now because it is always something we have to worry about." I think Sam's successors should listen to his words.

*   *   *

Freed by the span of uncontrol, the spiritual manager can focus energy on the cohesive elements that bring and keep the group together, a common vision and the spiritual practices that will support and encourage all members of the unit.

To assist in the discernment of the vision, to develop members to accomplish the vision and to always be present to encourage, support and, through personal example, lead them in a spiritual practice of being open to the universal spirit in the work place through meditation, trust in their shared intuitive directions, and belief in each other's inherent goodness is the vital function of the manager in the spiritually based organization.

~~~ ❧ ᚱ ~~~

CHAPTER SEVEN

Belief In People: Theory Y[4]

Theory Y[4]. I suppose most everyone is familiar with the work of Douglas McGregor's Theory X and Theory Y model. In *The Human Side of Enterprise*, McGregor in 1960 contrasted the traditional view of workers which he called Theory X with a much more optimistic set of assumptions about people which he called Theory Y.[1] Let's just take a minute to review those Theory Y assumptions. They are:

1. The expenditure of physical and mental effort is as natural as play or risk.

2. External control and threat of punishment are not the only means of bringing about effort through organizational objectives. People will exercise self control in the service of objectives to which they are committed.

3. Commitment to objectives is dependent on rewards associated with their achievement. The most important rewards are those that satisfy needs for self respect and personal improvement.

4. The average human being learns under proper conditions not only to accept but to seek responsibility.

5. The capacity to exercise a relatively high degree of imagination, ingenuity, and creativity in the solution of organizational problems is widely not narrowly distributed in the population.

6. Under the conditions of modern industrial life, the intellectual potentialities of the average human being are only partially utilized.

Reflecting on McGregor's theory, managerial expert Albert Robinson stated, "The focus of a Y manager is on the person as a growing, developing, learning being... allows people to test the limits of their capabilities and uses errors for learning... structures work so that an employee can have a sense of accomplishment and personal growth... motivation comes from work itself..."[2]

Spiritual managers not only believe these assumptions about people, but their belief is much stronger than you might ordinarily expect. Theory Y to a factor of 4. Four reasons for their belief in their community members:

1. The belief in the universal creator. All things, all matter are one in the spirit. All things are interconnected in this universe, in this one body. They are one inasmuch as they have been created by a common power, a common source. Because of this belief in a common spiritual heritage, the spiritual manager has more than a high regard for fellow living beings and the universe itself, she has a reverence.

2. Karma or "As you sow, so shall you reap" or "Do unto others as you would have others do unto you" teaches whatever I give off to others I will receive back. Therefore, if I wish to be treated as if I am responsible and creative, and have potential to contribute to my organization, then I must obviously treat others the same way. All of our behavior comes back to us, sooner or later.

3. Reality is what I believe it is. As the years have gone by I have come to believe more and more that I do create my own reality. What I believe I see, I see. What I constantly think or obsess about will have an overpowering force in my life and will become real for me. Therefore, what I believe about others is what

others will be to me. If I have a certain set of assumptions about people, they will be those kinds of people. Very few things in life are truly black or white. Most are some shade within those extreme hues, yet we have a tendency to see black or white. We will see those things that reinforce our beliefs and discount or simply not see those things which do not. Joel Barker's wonderful discussion of the power of paradigms shows how the Swiss lost the world's watch market because the quartz watch, which they invented, did not meet their paradigm of how a watch should work, so the Japanese and Americans, unburdened with the Swiss watch paradigm, picked up the patent and the rest is history.[3] The power we have in our minds to create our own reality is endless and spiritual managers carefully monitor their own perceptions by consciously testing what they see as reality against their belief in the universe and all life within it.

Perhaps this whole area is best summarized by physicist Gary Zukav, author of *The Seat of the Soul*. In discussing the evolution of our spiritual beings, Zukav talks about:

"the reality of each individual is created by his or her intentions and the intentions of others. What we think of as a physical reality that we share is an intermingling or a formation, a massive overlay of appropriate realities. It is a fluid, massive consciousness in which each of us exists independently of each other and yet coexists interdependently with each other. There is a oneness, a commonness between us and we need to know that our intentions or our perceptions of reality create reality for us and our perceptions of who we are."[4]

Therefore, as spiritual managers we see good in people and it becomes our reality.

4. The exception does not make the rule. How many times have we heard the old cliche about the exception making the rule and despairingly acknowledge its truthfulness? One employee acts up or is tardy for work and so what do we do? We promulgate a set of rules and regulations to control the behavior of everyone. The exception makes the rule. James Autry in his highly recommended book and video, "For Love and Profit," makes it clear that's not the way it should be.[5] There are exceptions. There are going to be people in our work force who do not share our vision, do not have a common belief system with us, have their own agenda and their own things they have to do. This is not a matter of being a good person or a bad person. It is just a matter of being a different person. What we need to do is to help them do what they need to do with us or perhaps without us, but we don't need to treat everyone as if they were "bad actors" because we have one or two exceptions in our work force. We need to deal with those exceptions and continue to have Theory Y[4] assumptions about all of our people, to ensure their full development and our unit's full potential.

*   *   *

But there are exceptions, "bad actors." What should we do then? We must be most careful in defining a "bad actor." Remember, we have no real knowledge of what the outcome of our actions is supposed to be, only what we sense it is supposed to be. This "bad actor" may have a more accurate sense of the intended outcome. She may be right where we are wrong. So use much reflection and meditation, and make sure to involve the individual deeply before taking any action.

*   *   *

Of course, understanding the importance of treating people as spiritual equals in human relations isn't exactly new. Let's turn for a second to the work of Plato's *Republic* written in 534 BC. In discussing the topic of "justice is profitable," Plato says:

> ...we intend that the subject should be governed...
> on the same principle as his superior, who is himself
> governed by the divine element within him. It is bet-
> ter for everyone, we believe, to be subject to a power
> of god-like wisdom residing within himself or, failing
> that, imposed from without in order that all of us be-
> ing under one guidance may be so far as possible equal
> and united.[6]

Much of our problem today is outlined by Toffler in *Power Shift* in describing the evolution of management principles.[7] It comes from the downfall of the tradesmen, independent farmer, businessman becoming employees in the industrial revolution with the consequent development of scientific management which basically saw people as very limited in their abilities to understand or to perform independently without high levels of control. However, even though it has taken some time since 1960, management today has recognized the need to change its management paradigm.

In *Principle-Centered Leadership* Steven Covey also traces the evolution of management paradigms from scientific management to human relations to human resource to what he calls principle-centered leadership. Each of these paradigms meets certain needs in terms of the individual.

Scientific authoritarian, as he calls it, meets a physical economic need. You get a job, you get paid and you can support yourself and your family. The human relations or benevolent authoritarian paradigm meets one's social or emotional needs where we deal with people's feelings and understand the use of kindness, courtesy, civility, and decency. The human resource movement cares about people and their contribution. It sees people as having minds and "with this larger understanding of man's nature we begin to make better use of their talent, creativity, resourcefulness, ingenuity and imagination." Finally, in discussing the principle-centered leadership paradigm, he says,

> We now go beyond the economic, social and psychological needs. We now see people as "spiritual beings." They want meaning. A sense of doing something that matters... Using this paradigm we manage people by a set of proven principles. These principles are the natural laws and governing social values that have characterized every great society, every responsible civilization over the centuries. They surface in the form of values, ideals, norms and teachings that uplift, ennoble, fulfill, empower, and inspire.

He concludes by pointing out his belief that the principle-centered leadership paradigm not only "embraces the principles of fairness and kindness and makes better use of the talents of people for increased efficiency, but also leads to quantum leaps in personal and organizational effectiveness."

In Covey's extensive study of effective leaders, one of the characteristics he identified is that such leaders really believe in people. "They realize that behavior and potential are two different things. They believe in the unseen potential of all people. They feel grateful for their blessings and feel naturally to compassionately forgive and forget the offenses of others... They refuse to label other people, to stereotype, categorize and prejudge."[8]

In his new book, *Empires of the Mind,* Dennis Waitley talks of the "new employee paradigm." This, he suggests, is how employees themselves look at and have developed a new team culture. It includes,

- autonomy and empowerment — minimum supervision, maximum training.
- meaningful work — environmentally safe with a mission to help society
- career path — opportunity to grow and move up the ladder
- incentives — compensation based on performance standards
- flexible schedule — consideration of family and cultural pursuits
- team leader — able to be a stand-out while remaining a team player.

While not all employees strive for all of these new paradigms as outlined by Waitley, I think it is safe to say that a spiritual manager recognizes the need of employees to have one or more of those characteristics in their work; otherwise they might, as Waitley says, "exercise their free agent rights and join another team that does have the vision, culture, synergy and leadership to win. A team, in short, that has embraced the new culture."[9]

*   *   *

A core characteristic of the spiritual manager is a deeply held belief in the inherent goodness of people and consistent action towards people based on that belief. But what is that action? What, specifically, do spiritual managers do? What is their role in a spiritually based work place?

CHAPTER EIGHT

Call To Serve: The Washing Of The Feet

<u>The Role Of The Spiritual Manager</u>

Okay, we're not running the universe, or even this little part of it called work. We're just doing our best one day at a time to do what seems like the right thing to do today.

Organizations are relatively horizontal consisting of small self-directed groups of individuals working together to accomplish their shared vision. Direction is supplied by managers and co-workers alike, each sharing their view of the vision and the results necessary to achieve success. Managers participate in the selection and development of workers with great belief in their inherent ability and desire to help them achieve their potential. Well, that's fine but that's only some of what we do. Bottom line, what is the manager's job anyway?

* * *

It can be recalled that our position regarding an organization is the only reason for an organization to exist is to facilitate the ability of the worker to fulfill the mission by creating and delivering needed goods and services to the firm's customers. However, we all know organizations don't do anything. People do. In this case, managers do. The way an organization facilitates the ability of its workers to produce the goods and services the customers need and want is through the manager. The manager's role is to serve the workers to make sure they have the authority, resources, knowledge, and in short, anything they need to have in order to serve the needs of the customer.

In the Forward to Kouzes' and Posner's new book *Credibility*, Tom Peters paraphrases one of the author's primary proposals, stating, "We believe that the old hierarchy is hollow. In other words, there is no way to move forward in today's violently competitive, fast-paced market by using the old structures." It is "liberate the leader in everyone" as Kouzes and Posner put it or else. "Enlightened managers," they add, "knowing that serving and supporting unleashes much more energy, talent and commitment than commanding and controlling."[1]

In *Reengineering Management - The Mandate for New Leadership,* James Champy concludes by pointing out that we are now in a second managerial revolution. "The first was about a transfer of power. This one is about an access of freedom." He goes on to say:

> It is the freedom at the center of the paradox of power: that the best way to get is to let go. It's freedom at the heart of the dispersal of authority and accountability out to where the customers are. It is the freedom to get out there ourselves. It's the freedom without which we can never summon the ideas and images we need to meet the demands and opportunities of our markets. And it is more obvious sorts of freedom too: freedom from stifling hierarchies, from organizational 'slots' and 'boxes'... free markets need free men and women to invent the future.[2]

An audio tape I listened to recently, *The Ten Commandments of*

Business and How To Break Them, by Bill Fromm, really hit the nail on the head. Fromm's position is that one of the commandments that needs to be broken is that the customer is king; when it comes to managers, the customer is not king. The employee is king. How can you expect employees to treat customers like kings if they themselves are treated like slaves. If you want your customer to be treated like a king, then you need to treat your employees like kings. That's your job as a manager, Fromm maintains, and I agree.[3]

Total quality management (TQM) gurus say the same thing. I recall going to a seminar some time ago where the speaker representing a firm working with a large number of *Fortune 500* companies pointed out that TQM turns the organizational chart upside-down. Instead of the worker trying to carry the load of layer upon layer of management, TQM changes the entire focus of the organization so that externally the most important person to the organization is the customer and internally the most important person is the individual employee member serving that customer.

Management's "customers" are those employees and they are there to consistently meet their customers' needs, i.e. their employees' needs, in order to produce the goods and services and to fulfill the mission of the organization.

We may remember that the job of the spiritual manager, like any other manager, is to get results with people and that continues to be true here. However, instead of directing, controlling, being in charge and making sure that people do what they are supposed to do, the spiritual manager has a different role.

The role is of servant. It is a paradox yet a truism nonetheless that the most effective leaders are those who put the welfare of the followers first and will do everything they possibly can to make sure those followers are safe, empowered and free to use their skills and talents in the accomplishment of their shared objective. The powerful ritual of the washing of the feet of the disciples by Christ created a model for us.

The modern management literature is full of references to this point. James Champy points out the paradox of power: **"The more you give away, the more you get... You give up control,"** he says, **"not power."**[4] But the power the modern new age manager has is given to her by the employees, not the organization.

One of the characteristics of principle-centered leaders, according to Covey, is that they see life as a mission not as a career. Their nurturing sources have armed and prepared them for service. In effect, every morning they yoke up and put on the harness of service thinking of others.

That image of "yoking up," literally putting a harness on yourself and sharing that harness with another person and the two of you pulling together to accomplish a task brought back the images of a horse-pulling contest I happened upon one day in rural Wisconsin. It was really interesting watching these horses pulling this large sleigh weighed down with massive amounts of concrete. I particularly noticed one handsome black that really stood out from the rest. His partner, sort of dull dappled grey, didn't look very good but between the two of them they managed time after time to accomplish their task and to pull their weight. As the weights got heavier and heavier, you could see the strain starting to show and finally at a very heavy weight when they were close to the end of the competition, they both charged out of their starting blocks only to hit the impasse of that tremendous amount of weight and an amazing thing happened. That beautiful black stallion quit. You could just see his effort diminish as he fell back and his share of the load was shifted to that old dappled grey. The grey didn't quit and kept on putting up even extra effort to pull the load so that within a few seconds the black, seeing the effort, got back into the game and they completed their task. I see managers in that kind of role. Solid, steady, strong, being there when we are really needed. Helping our co-workers to overcome seemingly impossible obstacles. Yet being fully willing to have the employee be the star, look good, get the recognition as long as the task for which we both have accountability is accomplished.

Covey goes on to describe a key issue in our ability to serve, the issue of trust. He asks, "If you have no or low trust, how are you going to manage people? When you don't have trust you have to control people. But if you have high trust, how do you manage people? You don't supervise them — they supervise themselves. You become a source of help."[5]

Another source looks at this issue of serving from a different angle. In *The Little Prince,* by Antoine de Saint Exupry, the Little Prince, as you may recall, was from another planet and was searching for his rose. When he came upon the fox, he learned an important lesson. "Men have forgotten this truth," said the fox. "But you must not forget it. You have become responsible forever for what you have tamed. You are responsible for your rose...." You managers are responsible to those entrusted to you. Their health, their welfare, their ability, their skills, their talents — all the gifts they bring to you. You are responsible to them. You are responsible forever for what you have tamed. In parting, the fox said to the Little Prince, "And now here is my secret, a very simple secret: it is only with the heart that one can see rightly; what is essential is invisible to the eye."[6]

This beautiful little story tells me that as managers we not only have a responsibility to the people in our organization to serve them but we need to go beyond the obvious. We need to manage with the heart as well as the mind. To me this means not using the typical means of control, such as managing by objectives, performance appraisals and the like, but really getting to know each and every individual and being able to understand in your heart what will bring about true joy and satisfaction in his life, and doing everything you can to assure that he has the resources necessary to bring those dreams into a reality, as well as the dreams of your shared vision.

Dennis Waitley purports that "the new global leaders will be people who can transmit knowledge and power to each member of an organization." He sees "...using this new empowerment to build empires in their minds offering vast inner and material rewards."[7]

*   *   *

Specifically, we have seen that one of the primary roles of the spiritual manager is to focus on, articulate, and to facilitate the ability of the worker to create and to share the vision. As the spiritual manager, he must gently lead the group in working towards its common objective. They do that not through power and coercion but by creating a safe environment, pointing out behavior that seems inconsistent with the vision, examining those behaviors and sharing new insights.

What else does the manager need to do? How else can we affirm the manager's role and responsibility to support the work force?

I've heard of a former commander of West Point who wanted his graduates to get egos out of the way and to learn how to be a servant to the troops.[8] Some evidence of its veracity are the officers of today's modern military. They know that their job is to make sure the soldier on the front lines has the resources, information and ability necessary to accomplish the mission. They are there to serve the troops.

While there is a top-down approach, *The Leadership Challenge,* by Kouzes and Posner, gives some good information to support the effectiveness of the managers serving their employees. "Many leaders don't just give lip service to the common business refrain, 'People are our most important resource.' They really believe in their human resources and utilize them to the fullest extent possible; and in the process 'grow people' and use their own power to transform their followers into leaders." They cited the work of Arnold Tannenbaum and his associates' research which showed "one vital lesson that all leaders should take to heart; the more people believe that they can influence and control the organization, the greater organizational effectiveness and member satisfaction will be." The authors studied a nationwide insurance company trying to account for the difference in branch office effectiveness. After controlling for financial and environmental factors, they found that "the sense of being able to influence what was going on in their own offices — was the most significant factor in explaining differences between high and low performing branch offices." The more power the employees had to determine the affairs of their branch, the better performance that branch had. The authors cite one of my favorite quotes from Rosabeth Moss Kantor, "Powerlessness corrupts and absolute powerlessness corrupts absolutely." This reversal of Lord Atkins' observation serves well to understand negative and destructive behavior in organizations. It is the antithesis of what spiritual managers really want to have in their organization. There is a lot of good material in *The Leadership Challenge* and I suggest you read it. My only problem is that they discuss these areas in a condescending way as though we are doing something for the employees which is inherently theirs as a natural right as fellow human beings and members of our universe.[9]

They, the workers, are the ones who are producing the goods and services that fulfill the mission. The manager's job is to use all his skills, talents and abilities to make sure they have the resources, the power, the freedom, the opportunity to use their many abilities in accomplishing their work unit's objectives. In other words, they are there to serve the worker, not to master the worker.

Another successful business leader who speaks eloquently of the role of servant manager is Max De Pree, chairman and former CEO of highly regarded Fortune 500 Herman Miller Co. As his audio tape *Leadership Jazz* points out, Herman Miller was practicing new age management long before most modern management gurus began talking about it. The results speak for themselves; highly profitable, innovative and sound results. When a production worker told him of a firing of two young managers by a corporate vice-president, De Pree opined to himself that the VP "must have lost his bearings" and supported the request of his workers to reinstate the supportive first line managers. "Leaders don't meet the needs of our customers," he says. "Followers (the work force) do." He, like so many outstanding leaders in government and industry, see the function of management to discern organizational mission and vision and to support the troops in their ability to carry out that mission.[10]

You can see examples of this whenever you see effective leadership where people really know and believe at a core level that the boss really cares about them as human beings and will do everything she can to help them get the job done. Maslow spoke of managers being barriers between employees and their natural needs. A spiritual manager is not a barrier. He or she is a facilitator, a conduit, a means by which those natural needs can be met and everyone — the organization, the worker and the manager — can benefit.

An early and profound thinker on this subject was Robert K. Greenleaf. His book, *The Leader As Servant,* has been cited by many of the authors cited in this book. Fortunately, his private writings have been collected and published by Don M. Frick and Larry C. Spears in *On Becoming a Servant Leader.* In their introduction the authors cite Greenleaf's Servant-Leader idea. "The servant-leader is servant first... It begins with the natural feeling that one wants to serve, to serve first. Then conscious choice brings one to aspire to lead... The difference manifests itself in the care taken by the servant — first to make sure that other people's highest-priority needs are being served. The best test, and the most difficult to administer, is: Do those served grow as persons? Do they (while being served), become healthier, wiser, freer, more autonomous, more likely themselves to become servants?"[11] I urge you to read the book for yourself. Many very successful people have and benefited greatly.

*　　　*　　　*

I have not spoken of traditional management issues like motivation, coaching and counseling, performance appraisal and the like. Nor do I intend to. However, the area of delegation, which assumes that one has authority he or she can give to others, needs to be commented on. Authority, the organizational right to do what is necessary to fulfill the mission should be inherent in every member of a healthy organization. All members have authority. You can't give it to them. You can try to keep them from exercising it but you can't give it to them. Work and work planning needs to be done but it is done with the workers, not for them. Common goals and objectives are reflected upon, statements of intent for what we hope to accomplish and benefits we intend to provide to our customers are discussed.

The individual with the support and needed assistance of her managers and teammates then proceeds to do what it is necessary to accomplish the task, constantly evaluating the process and trying to do it better. Each member has the desire, the goal and the authority to try to do it better, as well as somebody who believes in them and their ability.

The manager assists the process as facilitator, coach, and servant. Zukav has said that intentions determine reality.[11] If I intend to be servant, I will be servant, I will be seen as servant, and that will be the reality. If my intentions are to be master and I try to cloak them with servile behavior, the sham will be seen and I will be branded as the hypocrite I am.

In *Thriving on Chaos*, Tom Peters really deals with what he calls the "chief control tools":

> When Peter Drucker "invented" MBO (managing by objectives) in 1954 in *The Practice of Management,* he never capitalized the words nor did he use the three

words by themselves. He spoke of 'management by objectives and self control' — that is, non-bureaucratic self management was the avowed purpose. The antithesis, an accountant-driven, extra layer of bureaucracy was what usually ensued as the fine idea became encumbered over time by complex top-down techniques.

Teaching people how to do effective work planning and to set meaningful goals for themselves is one thing. Using MBO as a club to coerce them into doing what it is that management has determined needs to be done, is yet another. The latter definitely is not spiritual management.

*   *   *

Peters goes on to outline a number of steps to deal with control issues in the organization which are well worth reading. One of those is "fight conventional wisdom in one last way — allow stellar professionals (salespersons, engineers) to outearn, sometimes by a wide margin, their bosses."[12] I entirely agree with Peters' premise; however, I don't think that the possibility of outearning your boss should be limited to a very narrow range of employees. Every employee should have the opportunity to make more money than their boss. Compensation is about value, not position. I appreciate Peters bringing up this issue of compensation.

I don't like talking about compensation. Having had real problems with money over my lifetime, money issues still create some emotional barriers for me.

It would be easy and much more convenient to skip over getting paid as a spiritual manager. Manager's pay is not something I find a great deal of information on when it comes to management texts or styles.

Jesus didn't seem to put much store in compensation. His story of the workers in the vineyard seems to tell of a rather arbitrary approach, paying those who worked the last hour the same as those who worked all day. The point, as long as you receive what you bargained for, what difference is it to you what others are paid. This lack of concern for money is shown in the early followers who, according to Acts 2, 44-45. "All the believers continued together in close fellowship and shared their belongings with one another. They would sell their property and possessions, and distribute the money among all, according to what each one needed."[13] This sense of community and compensation (not Communism, a failed economic theory) puts money in its proper perspective in a spiritual workplace.

Compensation for the spiritual manager is not a major issue. There is a quality of fairness that needs to be taken into account. We need to have a wage that meets our needs and reflects our contributions to the organization in meeting our shared vision and be happy that's out of the way so we can concentrate on the work.

One approach to compensation is in a little monograph by Robert W. Rogers called the "Psychological Contract of Trust - Trust Development in the 90's Workplace." Rogers outlines an approach to try to create a fair rather than manipulative compensation system.

Its primary characteristics are: 1) be open with salary ranges so there are high levels of information about what people get paid in the organization; 2) make merit pay decisions based on fair objective data that reflect actual performance levels; 3) if you are providing a bonus, make sure it's quantifiable rather than discretionary or unilateral, and remember if you regularly give bonuses, you really aren't giving bonuses but just salary in a different form; 4) make sure that you have equity between same or similar jobs in the organization; and 5) make sure that compensation is competitive in the external marketplace.[14]

If I really believe that my job is to serve the employees, to help them become the best that they can be and to continually enhance their ability to help us accomplish our shared mission, then my expectation of compensation should not be a major issue. It's entirely reasonable to expect that a competent employee who makes major contributions to the accomplishment of our vision could well make more than I do. What difference does it make? I choose to go into management because it is that area where I can use my strengths and my skills in the highest and best fashion possible to accomplish the vision. Others have different strengths and skills.

Compensation should be fair and reasonably uniform, and reflect a reasonable and a suitable cost the enterprise can bear in the accomplishment of its vision. There shouldn't be a big discrepancy between any class of employees. I was sorry to see Ben Cohen, one of the co-founders of Ben & Jerry's Ice Cream, recently announce the job had gotten too big for them and that they were going to be advertising for a chief executive officer. Of course, they did so in their usual unique and creative ways, but the thing that made me feel sad inside was their realization that, in hiring a high-powered CEO (who has since departed), they were probably going to have to waive their seven times rule. You see, they had a rule that no one in the corporation could make more than seven times the lowest paid person in the organization. But looking at the possibility of hiring a highly skilled, competent business school trained CEO, they realized that they were going to have to violate that rule and join the ranks of most other major American organizations in creating huge and absolutely unjustifiable differences in compensation levels. Max Du Pree says Herman Miller has a 20 times rule which is modest compared to national trends.[15] "In 1965, CEOs made 44 times as much as an average worker; by 1995, the figure was 212."[16] In general, I don't think we have yet learned that the greatest excess baggage in organizations is located nearer the top than the bottom of the organization and to compound that with these exaggerated, inflated salaries is even worse.

In their thought provoking book, *The Soul of Economies, Spiritual Evolution Goes to the Marketplace,* Breton and Largent contrast two economic philosophies, those of the traditional "billiard-ball," where the economy is seen as fragmented, characterized by scarcity and competition for resources versus the "whole-seeking" or holistic view which is characterized by interdependency, reliance on creativity to create new resources and cooperative actions. In compensation patterns we can see much evidence of their billiard-ball, zero sum, win-lose analogy with the holistic win-win approaches being advocated by enlightened evolving management. In discussing greed, the authors cite Adam Smith in concluding: "economic health can't be separated from the aspirations of individuals, and there aspirations must go beyond selfish gain."[17] I recommend this book highly to give you a comprehensive view of economics and the spiritual style of management.

What is important is ownership. I am not talking about the phony sense of "ownership" that so many management gurus talk about today. I am talking about real stock ownership. Employees who share the vision and are committed to the accomplishment of that vision are entitled to and deserve to share in the benefits of accomplishing that vision. They take the risks by offering their time, talents and effort, and they deserve to get some share of the benefit. So any effort that can be made to make ownership available to everyone in the organization equitably should be made. What we do now is so bad. We have these exaggerated differences in salary structure, we then compound that by giving percentage increases, not flat increases which would tend to level them out, but percentage increases which make the differences even greater. Then we make stock available to people based on compensation. It is just bad. I have nothing against making money and believe the spiritual managers will use money just as they use their other talents, to help others. But the ego driven need to make so much more than anyone else is greed and greed is not a characteristic of a spiritual style of management.

*   *   *

At a very basic level this chapter is really about power. You may recall Toffler's discussion of the shift of power from the executive suite to the shop floor. Don't think either of us are talking about the kind of power struggles we knew when labor began organizing and workers were fighting to have some rights in their place of employment. Thankfully, we are well past those days and the need for that adversarial kind of relationship, for the most part, has passed. No, the kind of power shift that I envision could be better described as power sharing. An excellent discussion of the issue of power in the organization is in Scott Peck's book *A World Waiting To Be Born*. In his chapter "May God Have Mercy on You, the Civil Use of Power in Business," he uses McClelland's definition of power — "the capacity to influence others" — and points out that it "is almost by definition the most potent factor in organizational behavior. Incivility might simply be described as the misuse of power." He goes on to say:

> … the distinction has been drawn between spiritual power — the capacity to influence others by the loveliness of one's being — and political power — the capacity to influence others by one's money or dominant organizational position… It focuses on managers, the ones who possess the bulk of political power in business. Its thesis is that the spiritually incompetent manager will inevitably abuse her power. Consequently, its subject, the civil use of power in business, is the subject of the management as a high spiritual calling.

To illustrate his point, Peck cites the story of Jesus following his baptism and his sojourn in the desert and ultimate temptation by the devil. He points out that there are three temptations: to use power for food — money and security; to use it for spiritual flashiness; and the third to use it for the pleasure and glory of rulership.

The first moral he finds in the story is that Jesus, instead of going right to work as the Messiah, immediately went off on a spiritual retreat. I believe the spiritual manager will do likewise in some form or fashion. We managers need to take time before acting to seek our higher power's Will for us in a "retreat." That is, getting away from the work world for today and to empty ourselves out of the pressing concerns of that day and to focus instead on listening to what God's Will seems to be for us. Spiritual managers are constantly taking retreats, seeking to know God's Will for them and their organizations.

I remember having worked with George Romney, then president of American Motors, to get signatures to call a constitutional convention for the state of Michigan. Faced with a major decision as to whether or not to run for governor of that state, Romney went on his own spiritual retreat for 24 hours to seek God's Will for him in whether or not to leave his important position where he had accomplished an amazing turnaround of an almost defunct company in order to become the chief executive officer of an almost defunct state.

I recall when I was facing a dilemma of my own regarding the possibility of running for the U.S. Senate. I hadn't talked to Mr. Romney for years (having served as home headquarters chairman for the state of Wisconsin during his presidential bid), but when his wife Lenore answered the phone I told her briefly who I was and she said, "Oh, I am sure George would love to talk to you." And, sure enough, he came to the phone and shared his own experiences with me on what he went through in making that decision of whether or not to run. The main thing I remember from that conversation was to not worry about it. He pointed out that he didn't run for office until he was 55 years of age and, after all, I had a number of years to go before I was going to reach that time and if it was the right thing for me to do, I would know it. I would know it because I take the time to reflect on God's will for me through "spiritual retreats".

Another moral of the use of power as a manager has to do with seeking glory and power for power's sake. Peck points out that:

...the civil manager must ultimately empty himself of ambition. This is tricky. Those who have a vocation to power are naturally ambitious people. God would not call someone to leadership without giving him at least some taste for power. But before he can assume a position of leadership with full civility, the manager must refine this taste mildly. Defining ambition as the thirst for power for oneself, for one's own sake, he must then strip it away until all that is left is the thirst to be of service to others. Only then will the manager have become a true servant leader.

Finally, the third moral has to do with the temptations universal to power. One of those temptations I can readily identify with is what a good friend of mine calls grandiosity. The temptation to always appear grandiose — bigger than life, special, unique, different — is very strong in me. Humility, which I see as simply accepting myself for who and what I am with a sincere desire to improve, comes hard as I keep building fantasy castles in my mind. I could identify when the devil tempted Christ by challenging him to jump off of a tall building and to demonstrate that he was indeed God's son by having the angels come and lift him up. Hey, look at me, I am Christ. God's anointed one. Man, I could really go for that. After all, what would be wrong with that? That would just send a clear message out to the world so it would really listen to me. Right? Wrong. Most of my temptations to abuse power come from ego. That self-driven need to be seen as successful, better than, more accomplished than, brighter than, etc., etc. In response Peck says the point of civility, however, is power for the opportunity to be of service. He goes on to say, "The capacity to rise above temptation is the essence of freedom. One is simply not free to serve to do the right when one gives in to the temptation to stay in power… The civil manager must be prepared to quit her position or be fired at any moment." How to deal with all this? Peck says,

> It is the way of tension. The truly civil top manager will neither flee from the temptation nor succumb to it: instead she will live with it on a daily basis… She realizes she is both more and less than the business she manages. Less because its success is also dependent upon the optimal function of many others and she, herself, as its employee. More, because she knows that her loyalty to her own spiritual life is even greater than that to the organization.

Dr. Peck concludes "So we arrive at the great paradox of power: the only civil reason to seek power is to lose it, to give it away. The one mark above all else of the true servant leader is that she empowers others".[18]

*   *   *

I found for me that once I could get over my need to control everything in the environment, that the ability to serve others was still impeded by my ego. My willpower is a continuous barrier when I try to really focus on being a servant to others. Even in the classroom where I espouse this philosophy and usually practice it, every once in a while an irritating student will pop up who I would truly love to kill. At those times I find my willingness to be a servant disappearing and the old dominant do-it-or-else personality popping up to put this upstart in his place. All I can do when that happens is to recognize it, apologize for my behavior, and go back and say, "Now obviously there are some problems here. What can I do to help you with them?"

Of course, one major barrier to developing and carrying out the role of servant manager is fear, specifically fear of failure. If I or someone I work with "fails" there could be some severe repercussions. Because it is such a concern to so many, we should take a good look at how failure affects the spiritual manager.

CHAPTER NINE

Provides A Safe Environment: No Such Thing As Failure

Many managers assure people that there is no such thing as failure as long as we learn something from it. There is the story of the young executive who had made a serious mistake in his beginning executiveship and had cost his company $10 million. Fully expecting to get the ax, he got his resume out and began to think about other careers. When summoned to the chief executive's office, he was asked a series of questions about the incident, what happened, why it happened and what they could do different next time. Finally, not able to stand it any longer, the young executive said, "Boss, boss, don't you realize I just cost the company $10 million? Aren't you going to fire me?" The boss looked at him, smiled, and said, "Fire you? We just spent $10 million to educate you. Why in the world would we ever fire you?" You see, the point that we usually make is that failure, if it is part of our education and learning process, is really acceptable. As a matter of fact, we know that we have to have failure if we are ever going to succeed. But, despite the validity of that position, it still misses the point. The point is, there is no such thing as failure.

*   *   *

What is failure anyway? Failure is an action or behavior that we have taken that was designed to elicit a specific result which didn't elicit that result; therefore, we had a failure. You see, the point is that we determine what the result should be and, because we didn't get that result, we deemed the behavior a failure.

That's absolutely wrong. There is no such thing as failure. **In order to be a failure we have to know with certainty what the result is to be.** We don't know what the result is to be. We certainly have our guesstimates and our objectives and all the rest of the good stuff that we do to try to get some idea but the fact is that we don't know.

John Heider's wonderful little book, *The Tao of Leadership,* points out "because the wise leader has no expectations, no outcome can be called a failure. Paying attention, allowing a natural unfolding, and standing back most of the time, the leader sees the event arrive at a satisfactory conclusion."[1] My experience has shown me that the cause of much of my misery and my unhappiness with my self and others is my expectations of what should happen rather than my understanding and acceptance of what does happen.

How many "failures" have resulted in miraculous discoveries? The discovery of penicillin, the discovery of x-rays, etc. Mistakes, failures, some experiment that did not work out the way it was supposed to and yet there was an observant experimenter who turned that "failure" into discovery by being open to something that they did not anticipate, a result they hadn't planned. You see, these failures may be exactly what is supposed to be happening. We don't know.

In our efforts to become scientific managers we engage in management by objectives and our goal-setting process. We measure and calibrate, we qualify and quantify all kinds of actions and activities and results trying to come up with a reasonably good plan as to what we should be producing in any given time period. You see, these efforts are just our futile way to try to predict or control outcomes. If for some reason or other, and there could be countless reasons, none of which may have anything at all to do with the individual's capability, those results are not obtained then we have a failure, unsatisfactory performance, investor downgrading the value of our stocks and plenty of shame to go around. How futile all this is when we really look at our place in the universe and understand the minuscule impact of our performance and how powerless we are over that performance when related to the omnipotent power that permeates the universe.

W. Edwards Deming, who led the quality revolution in Japan and in the United States, had no use for managing by objectives. He saw it for what it was, an attempt on the part of management to control workers and to take from them the freedom to use their talents and abilities to produce what they knew far better than management could be produced.

Instead, Deming put his emphasis on the present moment, the here and the now, the process that we are working on to produce the goods and services that we strive for in our mission and vision. Rather than setting down arbitrary standards of performance, Deming emphasized us monitoring closely what it is that we do every day to produce our goods and services and to see how we could do it better. Rather than talking failure, today, managers talk PLAN, DO, CHECK, ACT.

PLAN... what are we trying to do here? How are we doing? Quantify your data. Develop a plan to do it better. Let's change this, let's try that. That's the plan. To DO. Let's go ahead and do it, try it out. See what happens. That's the CHECK. Check it out. Is it improving the goods and services that we deliver our customers? Is it enabling us to provide better quality at a lower cost? What is it doing? What do we know about it? Check it out. If it is fine, then ACT on it. Go ahead. Put it in. If it isn't, well Ok, that's fine. Let's go back to the drawing boards. We haven't lost anything.

The point is that Deming trained people not to get fixated on some far off objective but to constantly be looking at what they were doing everyday, to understand what they were doing and to be open to what it could teach them. If you ever met Deming or saw him on film, I am sure you would not consider him a spiritual manager. He was acerbic, critical, and judgmental of management in general. But he had many, many qualities of a spiritual manager. From what I could see, he had a deep and abiding faith in the workers, a tenacious focus on the present moment and on understanding and utilizing that present moment, or as he called it, the process, and a real openness to the lessons that life has to teach him and a willingness to stand up for those lessons. Finally, after many years and success in other countries, we have begun to follow some of his teachings. I really believe Deming would agree that there is no such thing as failure, other than closed mindedness, narrowness of vision and refusal to see the meaning in everything that happens in our life one day at a time.[2]

*   *   *

How many miracles have we walked by, looking at them as failures in our life? How many times have things not worked out the way we thought they should work out and, therefore, we didn't give them any credibility. Ask ourselves some fundamental questions like what is the purpose of this result, how can this result be used, why did this result happen anyway? There may be a reason for it and I need to understand that reason. Let's not be so tied down by this competitive driven culture that seeks to control, to predict, to force us into producing what is "supposed to be" produced. We are a wondrous creation directed by a loving and omnipotent power who cares deeply for us. We don't make mistakes. We don't make failures. And most importantly, we are not failures.

As spiritual managers we need to cast off all the old controls. We need to realize that we are a part of a huge ongoing process, look for ways to perform in that process and to always be open to, aware of, sensitive to what is happening, why it is happening, what the meaning could be behind that occurrence and what direction it might be giving us for our consequent behavior. If we pay attention to life, life will teach us. We don't make mistakes. There is no such thing as failure in a loving, caring universe directed by an omnipotent higher power. The only failure is to be closed to the messages, the direction, the insights, the intuitive feelings, the directions that are given to us by that power.

*   *   *

One of the ways failure raises its ugly head is in the annual, sadistic ritual of performance appraisals. Here, the manager, from his or her omnipotent throne, judges the performance of the workers and gives them feedback as to how they are doing and how they can improve. If a particularly enlightened manager, she may even ask how employees see themselves performing. But the real emphasis is on what the manager thinks, on the manager's judgment of the employee's performance.

The spiritual manager realizes that the only individual he can really understand sufficiently enough to begin to make any kind of judgments is himself and that truly appraising one's self is a difficult task. The spiritual manager carries on a continuous performance appraisal of herself, looking at how she is doing, evaluating her progress against what it is she is trying to accomplish, the kind of person she is attempting to become. This constant inventory-taking is the way in which spiritual managers strive to modify their behavior to truly become the type of individuals they are called to be. By taking their inventory, making the changes that they find necessary to make, they are modeling behavior for others to see. True performance appraisal cannot be made from outside of one's self. It can only be made from inside with a full examination of one's own behavior, the motives behind that behavior, and an understanding of what needs to be changed. I have always found in carrying out this activity for myself, that it is particularly beneficial to have a trusted friend with whom I share these inventories. His in depth knowledge of me and complete honesty with me helps me take a look at my behavior through his impartial eyes and compare that with what I see myself doing. I share my innermost insights, thoughts and concerns with him because I trust him and I know that he cares deeply for me and wants me to become the kind of person I want to be. Not what he wants me to be, but what I want to be.

So, too, with the spiritual manager. She can bring about real growth in the members of her unit by walking the walk, not judging people as failures, but by being open to all that happens and viewing it from the perspective of the shared vision. She gives feedback based on the shared vision and the person's own desired behavior. She realizes we are human, seeking progress, not perfection, in our spirited journey and in the work place.

*   *   *

By now, it is probably apparent that the central issue for the spiritual manager and the transforming organization is trust. Not only trust in the benevolence and wisdom of the power that guides the universe and us as elements in that universe, but trust in ourselves and in our fellows. The spiritual style of management cannot work in an atmosphere of distrust. People will not be willing to look into themselves and their own behavior, to exercise self-directing discipline and to monitor their performance towards the accomplishment of the organization's vision if they lack trust in the organization and its management. Inherent in the spiritual style of management is trust. Development Dimensions International's Robert W. Rogers excellent discussion of developing trust points out five fundamental strategies which need to be consistently and repeatedly exercised in order to create a high trust workplace for employees.

1. Create a high trust vision replacing traditional relationships, which tend to be turf-bound based on position, bureaucratic hierarchy and power and promoting self interest, with focusing on achiev-

ing common goals.

2. Know yourself — in the "early stages of building trust, frontline leaders must examine their own levels of trust in others and in their own trustworthiness. Do they have a fundamental belief in people or not? Knowing what one truly believes is the key starting point to understanding one's own behavior and making appropriate modifications." He goes on to point out that managers might be called to change ingrained habits that might have taken years to develop. They need to "look at themselves realistically and diagnose where they are demonstrating trust in others and where they are not. Then they need to develop a plan of action for continuously monitoring their behaviors to build on the positive trust-building behaviors they are exhibiting while minimizing or eliminating those behaviors that cause others to distrust them."

3. Emphasize the importance of honest, open and straight forward communication. Pointing out that "when leaders show respect, let people know they are listening, encourage involvement and share their thoughts, they are building strong bridges to support all trust-building efforts."

4. Model your beliefs, walk it! He points out that "leaders need to be able to walk the talk on trust by willingly discussing sensitive issues, admitting when they are wrong, expressing their own fears and anxieties, and doing more listening and less yelling and telling." When people see you walk the talk, then they believe and are willing to trust. However, "the hypocrisy of espousing one behavior and then exhibiting another is a prescription for disaster in creating an environment where trust becomes the predomi-

nant working relationship emotion."

5. Encouraging team trust where "team members are looking to each other rather than to the leader for support, praise and feedback. This positions leaders as coaches and mentors of self-led teams."[3]

Not only can the spiritual manager model that behavior for his workers but, in an environment of trust, he can become that friend, that spiritual advisor that people can come to and share their insights, knowing that they will not be judged a failure or given unsatisfactory performance ratings but instead will be given honest, direct feedback, lovingly and without any bias or ax to grind. After all, it is easy for the spiritual manager to do because he has the same objective the employee has, to help the employee to fully become everything she wishes to become in accomplishing the organization's vision and mission.

*   *   *

But sometimes that seems impossible. No matter what is done, obstacles keep getting in the way. This style of management, while simple at its core, isn't easy. Growth never is.

CHAPTER TEN

Challenges And Disciplines: Spiritual Isn't Soft

By now you are probably thinking what a whimpy deal this is. No control. Shared visions. No such thing as failure. I mean give me a break. Doesn't this guy know what it is like out there in the real world? You have to be tough. You have to be firm and hard with these people to get the job done; otherwise they will run all over you. Sound familiar? It certainly sounds familiar to me because that is what I believed for most of my life. Somehow or other I had to stay in control. Be tough. Be hard. Drive, push, get people to do what I wanted them to do.

Compared to that the spiritual style of management may seem soft but don't let it fool you. It is as tough as nails.

*   *   *

You may recall phrases such as "Many are called, few are chosen" or "The pathway to enlightenment is open to all but few persist." That just gives us some insight into the fact that the spiritual style of management is really very demanding on everyone. Both the manager and the members. Why is it so difficult? Because the drive to accomplish our vision comes from within us, not from without. If you are trying to get me to do something, I can develop all kinds of reasons and excuses not to do it. And if I am the manager trying to get you to do it, I can blame you and come up with lots of reasons why I wasn't getting the job done. But here the problem isn't explaining to somebody else why the job wasn't getting done, it is explaining to myself regardless of whether I am a manager or a member.

Let me give you some examples of experience with this management style and what it requires of people. In writing about Johnsonville foods, Tom Peters quoted one of their managers as saying:

> There's always this basic question when people hear about the Johnsonville way, hear about our dedication to people: they get it all mixed up. They think it is a real nice thing; that it is all fuzzy and warm. It is anything but that! It's far more difficult to work at Johnsonville than any other place. It takes a different class of person - a person who really wants to excel because nothing else is accepted. We are here to give you an opportunity to achieve whatever it is you want to achieve in life. We will also help you figure out what that is. We will give you the resources to do it. We are also going to give you a little push in that direction. But if you don't have a goal, if you don't see yourself as improving, you are not going to make it here. It is that simple. Because you are going to be letting down not only yourself but all your fellow workers...

He goes on to say:

> This is a way of life. You set the values that you cherish, that you will not deviate from. And then all of the other things flow from that. It's not that we put all

these things in and 'fix' all these people with all these new programs. It's just the opposite. We fix **me** and our values first, then all the rest happens.[1]

Toffler, in writing about the GE plant experience (where they greatly reduced the hierarchy and empowered the workers who, through committees of their own, made production scheduling and even hiring decisions), points out that, "some workers quit when this system was introduced explaining that they didn't want to carry the additional responsibility it entailed." But as a hopeful sign, he goes on to point out that "employee turnover has fallen from 15% in the first year of the new system's operation to 6% four years later."[2]

A wonderful example of the difficulty of the spiritual style of management for both the manager and the worker in a spiritual environment is that of Ghandi. In writing about *Ghandi, His Life and Message for the World*, Lewis Fisher points out that the key to Ghandi's achievement was "satyagraha." He explains "satya" means truth, the equivalent of love and both are attributes of the soul; "agraha" is firmness or force. "Satyagraha is therefore translated soul force." Ghandi wrote, "It is the vindication of truth not by the inflicting of suffering on the opponent but on one's self."

Fisher points out that "satyagraha reverses the "eye for an eye" policy which ends in making everybody blind or blind with fury. It returns good for evil until "the evildoer tires of evil." Ghandi showed that ordinary human beings were capable of high-mindedness even under very irritating circumstances and that is tough, not soft.[3]

*   *   *

The spiritual management style requires discipline, honesty, and commitment: From managers and employees. Think of something in your life you really want to accomplish. Something you really want to get done. Something really different than what you have been doing in the past. Take quitting smoking for instance. You know smoking is not good for you. You know you would be much better off if you could stop smoking. Yet it is really hard, isn't it? It requires a lot of honesty with yourself in terms of your addiction and your dependency on the nicotine. It requires discipline to develop a program that will work for you and to stick to that program day after day after day. And that requires commitment. And that's hard, not soft.

Let's take a more pertinent example, total quality management. Many people in organizations want what total quality management offers, increased quality and higher levels of employee morale, resulting in increased productivity. In these days of doing more with less, TQM seems highly desirable. Do we know it will work? Yes! Total quality management is nothing more than a packaging of time-proven management principles and certainly has been demonstrated in a small number of companies and in other economies as well. Yet, look at what's happened with the U.S. experience. Companies have started total quality management only to gradually erode employee empowerment or to revert to mandating program "improvements" from on high. An interesting study of three governmental agencies by Carolyn Ban showed mixed results and her conclusion that implementation of TQM requires "consistent, long-term management commitment. Without this commitment, the organization may do more harm than good by confirming the jaded view of many in government that TQM is nothing more than the latest management fad."[4]

Truly spiritual management requires the best of all of us, manager and worker alike and to our human nature, that isn't easy.

*   *   *

A manager's job is to get results with people. The spiritual management style is not an excuse for not producing results. If anything, it increases the level of commitment because the results being sought after are those which manifest themselves as coming from a source far greater than ourselves and from a belief that these results are part of an overall plan to create a better world, a better universe. So nonperformance can't be tolerated. People having problems in seeing the mission, fulfilling their role in the mission, need to be understood. Need to be treated gently. Need to be helped so that they can either perform or seek opportunities elsewhere where their skills and talents are better suited. But they must be dealt with. We are not talking about just not meeting some goal here. We are talking about not fulfilling our vision, not accomplishing that value that we hold to be so important in our lives. And to do that we can't be soft. We have to remember we are not running the show. We are not dealing with these performance problems out of some inner deficiency we have leading to abuse of power or to just look good in the eyes of higher management. We and our members share a vision. We have a common belief in the values we hold. We are simply doing our job by helping those folks who are having difficulty in doing what it is they are supposed to be doing. We should be fair and gentle, yes, but firm nonetheless. After all, loving firmness is called for.

My study of spiritual leaders clearly demonstrates their spiritual firmness. It has been pointed out to me that the only time Jesus demonstrated real anger was at the merchants using the church as a place of business. His anger and his firmness was not because someone was doing something to him, but because they were defiling his father's house. The importance of our vision, the importance of our values, and the importance of the individual who needs an opportunity to be fully productive in using her skills and talents and not wasting those skills and talents any unsuitable position, calls for firmness.

Compounding the difficulty of the spiritual style of management are conflicts that we seem to have with "the world." "The world" seems to have a set of perceptions about how things should be done that usually run pretty contrary to what we talk about in this book. I have a good friend who was up for a very high level position at Florida State University and one of the major knocks against him is that he is too "laissez-faire." He allows people to use their judgment and to do what they think is best. Having been his graduate assistant for two years, I know he is the kind of manager that brings the best out in people and for whom you will gladly work those extra hours and make the extra effort required to accomplish a task because it is a task that you have had a role in developing and for which you have a sense of responsibility in accomplishing. Yet, even though his peers recommended him, my friend did not get the appointment. "Results oriented" managers (as opposed to "people oriented" managers) often seem to be preferred when of course we need both orientations.

Then again, employees have to deal with the world as well. "Why do you expect this from all of us? Our friends who work for these other organizations don't have to do that. They are not involved in this. They are not expected to use their own initiative and judgment.

What happens if we make a mistake," etc. etc. They have lots of concern about not doing things the way others do it or being different. Then, too, there is the temptation to "get away with it." It is sort of like cheating on your income taxes. How are they going to know about it? "So what if I claim a little extra expense here; they aren't going to be able to catch me." That rationale, the temptation to be able to cut corners, cheat a little and get away with it seems to be part of what the world tells us is appropriate behavior, and here we are talking about being honest, responsible and committed. There is nobody breathing down your neck and checking out everything you do. But you know. Your co-workers know. And ultimately your results will show. But the bottom line is that you know and you can't do it even if the world says you are a dummy for playing ball with the boss. The spiritual style of managing is not easy, it is not soft for the manager or for the employees. It requires the very best.

Remember Tom Peters' talk of zealots, people obsessed with the need to fulfill their vision, accomplish the goals of the organization. He talked of these people in glowing terms and I can understand that today. At the same time, I still have a level of discomfort having been obsessed and driven to be successful for so long. Yet the idea of being a zealot, of being totally committed to our vision and whatever it requires to accomplish it is attractive to me. What I have come to believe for myself is I get in trouble when I fail to be open to challenges to that vision or only have one such vision. I need to have the courage to change, if the necessity for change is shown to me. I need to have the same level of commitment to my vision for my marriage, my children, my community, my God and myself.

We can, in fact I believe we have to, love others. Some don't make it easy. At times we may judge other's behaviors, resent their harmful actions aimed at us (or so we perceive). But that love, that reverence for, that cherishing of all life, is a very important part of who we are as spiritual managers. Yet love doesn't allow people to be less than they can be or to do less then they are capable of doing. Love exhorts us to be fully our very best selves. And if we see others falling short of what they want to do and are capable of doing, love calls us to intervene, to step in, to see what we can do to counsel them in resolving these problems.

The concept of tough love came home to me very personally. Our second son had had an ongoing problem with drugs in his life and my way of dealing with it had been mostly to ignore it until it became too real to ignore and then to punish the behavior. Well, that succeeded in driving him out of the home to the underground where he was eventually arrested for illegal possession of a controlled substance. A couple of years later our youngest son developed some of the same problems, only by then I had begun this spiritual journey which had really begun to change how I looked at life. This time I did not ignore the behavior. Nor did I punish the behavior. What I did instead was constantly call the behavior to my son's attention. Failing grades, getting kicked out of the school musical despite his magnificent voice, not doing well in athletics, all these symptoms were there and I would constantly call them to his attention. Just simply by saying, "This is not you. This isn't the same person who lettered in three major sports. This is not the same outgoing and personable leader of a very successful drum and bugle corps. This is not the honest, trustworthy son we have known for so many years." But never once did he doubt or should he have doubted that I loved him. I couldn't stand what he was doing to himself with these drugs, but I truly loved him and I hurt because he was hurting himself. Finally, after seeking some help on his own at school, he decided to go into a 28-day treatment program for his addiction. Today, even though like all of us he struggles with life and life's terms, I marvel at my son's internal stability, at the graces he seems to possess, and the tremendous quality of his character that has emerged. Incidently, the same is true of my second son who now has developed very strong helping skills and has recently been cited as the very best in his profession by his employer. I take no credit for any of this. The potential of my sons was there. It was always there. The only thing I might have done was to point out to them behavior that was inconsistent with their own qualities, their own goodness and give them an opportunity to do something about it.

No, the spiritual style of management is not soft. It is tough. It is firm, it is demanding because it is driven by a higher power through a common shared vision and comes from inside us, not to fill some sick need of dominance or power, but to fulfill a healthy need of helping our organization and helping others to become their very best selves.

CHAPTER ELEVEN

Seeks Worthwhile Work For Self And Others: "T.G.I.M."

As spiritual managers, we truly hate to see individuals waste their skills and talents, to not fully develop themselves to be their highest and best self. We will commit ourselves to and help that person work through whatever process is necessary to remove the barriers and the obstacles towards self-actualization.

Even as we treasure the individual becoming his highest and best self, so, too, do we treasure the organization being its highest and best self. Spiritual managers who observe or are part of an organization which is wasting itself on useless levels of hierarchy, tomes of redundant policies and procedures, or has major elements doing nothing but processing paperwork are alarmed, concerned. They feel an urge to change that structure to remove all this redundancy so every individual's work in that organization is directly related to accomplishing the organization's shared vision and goals.

Worthwhile work begins with the vision.

I have no idea what your vision should be like. I know that for myself any vision I strive for comes to me through my meditation, my intuitive contact with my higher power, and has certain qualities.

It will definitely be "soul" directed. It need not be logical, empirical, or justifiable in terms of the analytical standards the world likes to apply to such organizational processes. It is one that I feel within my inner self is appropriate and right, and I trust that inner judgment.

Secondly, this vision will give me some direction in answering the question, How will people, this world or this universe, be better off because we do what we do? I need to see that someone, someplace, something will be better because we are doing what this vision calls us to do. If not, then I don't believe it is appropriate for me.

Finally, not only do I see my vision in terms of how it will create a better world for our customers and will favorably impact the universe, but I need to see how it will favorably impact me and my employees. We need to be strengthened, we need to achieve personal growth and our vision should have an internal aspect to it that will enable us to accomplish our own personal goals, our personal visions, while at the same time creating a better world for others.

If I am engaged in work which does not meet these criteria, it is not worthwhile work for me and I have to separate myself from it. As a spiritual manager, I suggest that if we find our organizations doing things that are contrary to our vision then we need to separate our organization from these things.

*   *   *

A fascinating article from *AHP Perspective* discusses organizational transformation. In it Christian Forthomme says:

> organizational transformation is concerned with facilitating and allowing the emergence of a totally new state of being; with making things different — letting something totally new emerge from an old structure. It focuses on potential and spirit and individual development and transformation… It is more concerned

with creating collective intention than changing billing systems. OT is primarily concerned with purpose: Why do we do what we do? And with having a strong sense of personal purpose in the organization. What kind of work we do matters because it has to reflect our deepest internal drives and values. In order to be excellent or high performing people, we have to find an activity that reflects who we really are and want to become. OT is allowing both the individual and the organization to get more clear on their own sense of purpose.[1]

If we find ourselves toiling in organizations that lack vision, which are totally focused with changing billing systems and have no real sense of personal purpose, then we've got a problem and need to look at some of the principles of organizational transformation. Obviously this is not an easy job. Bruce Flynn speaks of "a collective change of perception by a group of people; spiritual, energizing, transformation leadership, visioning. It is not enough to have the manager change his or her mind or perception... when a whole group of people change their perceptions there is a 'leap'."[2] But if you find yourself in an organization where your best efforts to bring organizational transformation are doomed, then take hope because more and more small and medium sized American organizations are recognizing the validity of a spirit-based management system.

*   *   *

Equally important in terms of worthwhile work are the qualities of the job we do. Managers and workers alike must ask themselves, "Does this job contribute directly to the vision of the organization?" If it doesn't, then don't do it. Unnecessary reams of paperwork, layer upon layer of auditing and financial reporting and accounting, checks of every kind, controls upon controls. If it doesn't contribute directly to the vision, then don't do it.

For instance, if you are in personnel, ask yourself how your job contributes to the accomplishment of the vision of your organization. If you can't answer that question succinctly by showing that your organization is well staffed, trained, and focused and therefore more successful in accomplishing its vision, then you better change your personnel practices or get another job. If you consistently are vision-driven and base all your management behavior on the accomplishment of that vision while at the same time consistently working towards helping every single employee in achieving maximum self development, you are practicing a management form which will minimize legal liability and maximize your effectiveness in accomplishing the vision of your organization.

One thing is for sure, we do not need make-work jobs today. Those are nonproductive for everyone in our environment. They are too expensive to pay for, whether they are taxes, or the cost of goods or supplies. International competition, tremendous demand on resources, and legitimate ecological concerns all say that we need to make sure that we stay focused on our vision and that every person be helped to be the most effective she can be in accomplishing that vision.

*   *   *

Remember the movie *Field of Dreams?* Kevin Costner's character was told by an intuitive inner voice to build a baseball field in an Iowa cornfield. "If you do, they will come." He had a vision. A vision he came to share with a few others and the field was built. And he listened to that inner voice and they came. The baseball players from the past came and the public came. What's the moral of this story for the spiritual manager? Simply that if you listen to that inner voice you will achieve results. Things will happen. They will come together. You will be doing worthwhile work for you and for the world that you inhabit. Remember, not everybody came to the field. But enough came to the field to fulfill the vision. That's the point.

Let's take the automobile business. I spent my college days building Oldsmobiles at the Fisher Body Division in Lansing, Michigan. My dad and brother both retired from General Motors, Fisher Body Division. I have had some experience with the automobile business as an employee and as a buyer of its product. How do you suppose the topic of worthwhile work is viewed in the automobile business? What do you think the shared vision of managers and employees is in the automobile business? I know that when I was there there was not much of a vision at all. It was mostly dog-eat-dog, union against management, get the cars out no matter what shape they were in when they got off the assembly line, just get them out. That was the idea. And above all else do not ever let the line shut down. Well today, I am watching a new automobile company come about — still General Motors, but being run a whole different way. It is called the Saturn Division. They even located it away from typical automobile manufacturing sites, supposedly to create a new culture. Today, those workers building those Saturn automobiles have a different view of their job than I did. They have a vision of the kind of customer who will be buying their car and how their car will be viewed and used by that customer. They're involved with that car and they are involved with the customer, even to the point of inviting the customers to come back to visit with them, to talk to them about their car. You see, I don't think those employees at Saturn are just making cars. I think they have a vision, a vision of providing their customers with stylish, safe, efficient, quality transportation. They have a vision that shows up as you talk to people who bought Saturn and who talk about the tremendous service and feedback that they get when they buy their cars.

But you know, Saturn's vision may not be Mercedes Benz's vision or it may not be Nissan's vision. All organizations don't have to have identical visions. They listen to what seems right for them, for the benefits they want to provide and can be driven by those benefits, not those that others will provide.

In the 1970s, I learned a lot from Peter Drucker as I was part of an effort to totally reorganize and reorient the nation's sixth oldest life insurance company. He got us to be focused on our customer and to create a vision of what kind of organization we wanted to be to meet the needs of that customer. Today, Drucker still gives me insight. His recent article on organizational structure in the information age related an organization to a symphony organization.[3] In a symphony you have a hundred or so players and one conductor. The conductor and the players review the score, the raw material they have to work with. A good conductor and the players then search out and envision the final benefits they want to produce for their audience and themselves as they experience the joy of that creative art. The interpretation, the nuances, the feelings that should come out of that piece of music… together they create a vision of that beautiful piece of music they will create. The conductor's job is not to play the horn or oboe or violin, even though she may have that capability. The job is to focus the orchestra on that vision. To enunciate that vision, to bring the very best out of every single one of those players so that the vision can be accomplished and the audience be enthralled with the beauty of that musical form. The conductor has to be highly visible in communicating that vision. She has to be continuously vision focused and give feedback to the members of the orchestra on how they are doing in carrying out their part of that vision. She must be demanding, pointing out where performance is not consistent with what the player is capable of or should be doing and gently but firmly move the player along to the point where he can accomplish his potential and help fulfill the needs of the organization in meeting its own vision of that piece.

I have to tell a little story here. My editor strongly recommended I delete the symphony conductor illustration on the basis that most conductors are seen as tyrants and I shouldn't have that kind of a model in a book on spiritual management. Well, I was inclined to go along with her. She's very good and helped me a great deal with the book. Then came Aspen and Bobby McFerrin.

Having been in Denver on business, my friend Grantham Couch and I headed for Aspen where he was spending the summer. Knowing my strong preference for classical music, he mentioned a concert that evening and we agreed to go. Arriving right at the concert's beginning, I had no idea what the program was, only that the ticket cost $30.00, which I judged high for a summer tent concert.

Then bounding up to the podium came this slightish, casually dressed black man, hair in corntails, and the most radiant smile you've ever seen. And then ensued the most memorable concert I've ever attended. The music was rich, full, joyous. Beethoven had never sounded so uplifting and exhilarating before. The sophisticated Aspen audience gave round after round of standing applause, the orchestra beamed and basked in the thrill of their accomplishments. Fortunately, we had cheap seats, on the side of the tent where I could see Maestro McFerrin at work. Constantly smiling, encouraging, singing to this magnificent orchestra, he certainly brought out the best in them all and in the music they performed.

Overcome by the emotion of the entire evening, I had to find out what he might have done to elicit the musical peak performance. So I talked to the musicians, some first chairs of our nation's leading symphonies, others outstanding students from around the world. It was easy for they were all standing around excitedly talking to each other and friends, not packing up and heading for the exit as performers tend to do.

They told me he not only rehearsed them, but he shared his vision of the music and then asked them theirs. It was a collaborative effort, something from both conductor and performer, joined together in a celebration of creative equals. They were totally involved and empowered by the vision of the classics they loved and the conductor who showed he loved and respected them.

Next day's paper's interview gave one more insight. Here are some of his quotes: "The bottomline in conducting is the power of persuasion and to inspire musicians to play with all the fire and passion and joy and energy they have," said the highly articulate artist. "And I'm always open to hearing musical ideas from members of the orchestra because I don't know everything." Also, "Music is noncompetitive," he said. "It's a way of immediately creating a sense of community and collectivity. It's a transcendent dance that is spiritual art and spiritual affirmation. Music asks nothing and demands nothing." What tied it all together for me was his conclusion. "So many people are out there looking to find a spiritual experience," he said. "But every moment is a spiritual experience and it's up to us to use our time well... just living and trusting God." The article's conclusion, "So, don't worry. Be happy. The philosophizing music man has arrived," could be paraphrased to say the spiritual manager of an outstanding symphony orchestra has arrived.[4]

So there you have it. Drucker is validated. Spiritual management does exist in symphony form and the results speak volumes for what its potential is in any organization or as so aptly put by Ara Guzelimian, Aspen Music Festival artistic administrator: 'You light up the place, Bobby. Thank you.'

This whole issue of meaningful work goes beyond the work place. Work is inextricably woven into life. **We cannot hope for a meaningful life with meaningless work.** The two should be of one fabric complementing and supporting each other in our spiritual journey. As Toffler and others have pointed out, prior to the industrial revolution our work was a major and meaningful component of our life. Whether it was a trade or farming, it identified who or what we were and gave us opportunities for sense of achievement, pride, and satisfaction. Specialization and compartmentalization brought about by the industrial revolution destroyed that sense of pride in our work. Now we never see a finished product, only the little widget that we worked on. And the demand is not for quality, it is for production.

At my mother's funeral recently, I spent a good deal of time talking to my brother, a retired General Motors millwright and labor leader, and a number of his friends and our former neighbors, all of whom had retired from a factory environment. The overwhelming consensus of their remarks was that they got out of that job as soon as they could. They had spent 30 years tolerating that existence in order to provide for their families, but as soon as some other source of economic security was provided, they were out of there. It need not be that way. I talked to a couple of my friends who had been in the life insurance business with me for many, many years. These are truly professional life underwriters who focus on their clients and provide valuable services to their clients in helping them meet their financial needs and objectives. These men are still working and, even though they have more than adequate financial security and independence, plan on continuing to work. It gives meaning and satisfaction to their lives. They love what they do.

One of the best writers on this subject is Marsha Sinetar in her best seller, *Do What You Love, The Money Will Follow,* and in her more recent audio-tape, *Work as a Spiritual Path - How to Bring Joy and Meaning to Your Work Life.* Here she outlines approaches which will assist individuals seeking to achieve their life goals while honoring their spiritual beliefs as well. "Work becomes a devotion — a labor of love and... a spiritual exercise because the individual's concentrated powers, their choices and values, are motivated, prompted and fueled by love. And their service... is simply an enactment of this positive life force."[5]

Life and work can be such that we no longer look forward to

Friday, T.G.I.F. Instead we can cherish each day, workday or not, and can easily say, T.G.I.M., or …S or …W. Each day is special with its gifts of work and life.

*   *   *

Worthwhile work. We must demand worthwhile work. We deserve worthwhile work. What we do in our work lives is too much of our lives to be wasted. We cannot tolerate useless, worthless work in order to simply generate funds to do worthwhile things elsewhere. Worthwhile work is there. The potential for worthwhile work is in every valid organization and for every individual. We have a right to it and we should insist on it.

And, surprisingly, part of worthwhile work is nonwork. We need to have time in our work life for reflection, for meditation, for the quiet time to be one with our creator, that universal force, that higher power. We need our own personal vision and the balance necessary for a spiritual life. It's that continuous staying in touch with, listening to and responding to that voice we hear that is the basis for all spiritual management for both the manager and members. We need that quiet time and we should build it in so that we have opportunities to constantly be affirming, refining and, if necessary, redirecting our vision.

Worthwhile work, making sure the organization's vision speaks to our core values, making sure each individual in the organization has the opportunity to contribute fully to that vision and to fulfill their dreams, these are baseline requirements for the spiritual manager.

CHAPTER TWELVE

Seeks To Understand, Not To Be Just Understood: Manipulation Or Motivation

It seems like every book on management has something about motivation. While I don't want to spend time on a lot of basic management issues, motivation is one that particularly concerns me. If you go back and look at motivation, the old Theory X or scientific management approach was basically one of incentives and punishment. "Do what I want and I will give you a prize. Don't do what I want, and I will threaten you with your job. I'll get rid of you. I'll dock your pay. I'll do something to hurt you." That approach, usually called the carrot and stick approach, is still around in abundance not only in employer/employee relationships, but in parent/child relationships and lots of other places. I like the story I heard recently at a meeting. The speaker said that "If you seek to motivate people by using carrots or sticks, then you are basically treating them like jackasses. Why then be surprised if people act like jackasses?" This approach certainly does not practice the awe or the reverence for each individual I envision for a spiritual manager.

* * *

Of course, modern management theory recognized that was not an effective way to motivate people and, based on the work of Maslow and others, began to understand that true motivation comes from within people, not from without. Maslow's hierarchy of needs helped us begin to look at an individual in terms of where they were in their particular need level on the basis that, if we understood what they needed and that they could get what they needed by doing what it is that we wanted them to do, they would be motivated to do it. Not because we wanted them to do it, but because they would get what they needed by doing it. Sociologist Frederick Herzberg took the theory further by discovering that there were dissatisfiers or hygiene factors that existed in the work environment that needed to be cleaned up if we were to have a motivated work force. However, he cautions, dealing with these hygiene factors would not motivate an individual and we had to look at satisfiers or motivators such as recognition, achievement, personal growth, work itself, etc., if we truly wanted motivated people in our work force. Again, we have to know and understand the member and what it is that motivates them.

Harvard psychologist David McClelland took the motivational theory another step forward by synthesizing some of Maslow's hierarchy of needs into his basic social motivators — power, affiliation, and achievement — and by pointing out that every individual has some of these motivators but that one usually tends to be more dominant than the other. He then took an important further step by saying that the task of management is to align an individual's motivations with the requirements of the job so as to create a fit between the two so one's inherent motivators would naturally be met by doing what the job would call for.[1]

*   *   *

These intrinsic motivators exist in everyone and the job of management is to identify them so that members can get what they need to get out of the work experience by doing what needs to be done in the work place. This is all fine and good except for one small problem. Most managers today have simply replaced carrots and sticks with recognition, achievement, personal growth or what have you. They have substituted one form of reward, cash bonuses etc. with others and still use them to manipulate people to get them to do what it is that they want them to do. Let me give you an example. In their book, *The Leadership Challenge,* Kouzes and Posner start right out in part 1, page 1, with this quote from Vance Packard and *The Pyramid Climbers:* "Leadership appears to be the art to getting others to want to do something that you are convinced should be done."[2]

Stop and think for a minute about the true relationship between many managers and their employees. How many times have you heard, "we set up these quality circles to help our people feel like they have a say-so around here." Or "we have a recognition program to make people feel important." What are they really saying? People don't have a say-so, aren't really important. We all know who has the say-so, who is important and it's not them.

Implicit in many of these modern motivational management theories is the assumption that we, the managers, know better than or are superior to the worker and that we should use all of these techniques to get people to do what it is that we think they should do and what will be good for them if they do it. I don't think that is true. I don't think that I know more, or am in any way superior to an employee. We are all different but should be seen as equal in terms of our ability to produce goods and services that are called for in our vision. I don't need to develop some grand plan for this individual to get her to do what she should be doing. If as a manager I am open and free with all the information I have, if together we develop our vision, if together we determine our goals and the direction in which we wish to go and the ways in which we intend to try to accomplish that vision, if I provide training and support that the individual judges she needs to have to be able to perform at her peak level, I don't need to worry about motivating her or getting her to do what it is I want her to do. She knows what needs to be done. She is as committed to what needs to be done as I am and is as important to getting that done as I am, if not more so.

You are talking to a great collector of plaques. I have won more plaques for more things than most anybody I know. But as I really look at things today, from the viewpoint of a spiritual manager, I really see plaques, recognition, pats on the backs, attaboys, all that kind of stuff as some condescending form of approval which undermines and belies the true relationship I see between an employee and a manager.

As an example, praise, usually considered a motivational tool, is more often used as a means to reinforce the status of the hierarchy and keep workers in their place, according to Richard Farson in his challenging audio tape *Management of the Absurd.*[3] If we see ourselves as superior, needing to get "them" to do what it is we have decided "they" should do, then nearly anything we do from carrots and sticks to plaques is manipulation, not motivation.

*   *   *

In his discussion of power, Rollo May talks about five different forms of power: coercive, manipulative, competitive, nutrient, and integrative. And all, save the last, of these forms of power assume that one party has greater knowledge, ability, strength, skills than the others and either uses power to force, con, take on, or take care of the other person.[4] Only integrative power is a form of power that I use with another individual. Here I recognize I have power and so does the individual with whom I am in a relationship.

The task is not to have one's power dominate the other but to fully use both parties' power in the accomplishment of the task. This is the goal of the spiritual manager. To recognize the strengths, the talents, the power and the motivators of every single employee. What is it that motivates them? Recognize that, honor that, value that. That is part of the uniqueness that is that person. But our job is not to use that to manipulate; it is to make sure the individual is able to use that strength, that source of drive or motivation to accomplish the task to which we are all committed, the shared vision we are striving to accomplish.

I hear a lot of talk of empowerment today. And yet what I see is not true empowerment. I see little dibs and dabs of authority being given to people. Always, of course, with strings being attached. "If you don't do it right, I will take it back." That's not what I am talking about. That's not really motivating. I heard a General Motors lineworker on television some time ago talk about how things were going at General Motors. Of course they went through a quality revolution and instituted quality circles and all kinds of employee participatory plans but in effect this employee was saying that it's the same old story. They are the bosses. They call the shots. They may give little projects to do but even those have to get approval. It is the same old story.

*   *   *

You see, for me to think that I can motivate someone else means I have some power over that person. I don't have any power to change anybody. Only the individual can change herself, make the decision to do what it is that needs to be done. All the rest of this is nonsense. I may get token compliance. I may get somebody giving me some lipservice, but all the time they are undermining, sabotaging, denying, blocking, procrastinating and I am certainly not getting their peak performance.

Many years ago when he wrote his six points to create an environment of achievement, McClelland stressed the fact that the employee has to have a say so in the goals and objectives. The spiritual manager working together with the employees to develop a shared vision, working with each employee as a partner, coach, and counselor to help that member become the very best person he can become, truly provides an environment where an individual's natural motivators come to fore and drive him to share in the desire of all the workers to accomplish their common vision, mission and goals. True motivation recognizes, honors and respects each individual and what it is that motivates her and allows her free and open opportunity to use her skills, and to use that motivation to accomplish the organization's objectives. Use of those motivators to purposely get people to do what it is that managers have predetermined they should do smacks to me of manipulation, of puppets on strings and Svengalis in disguise.

CHAPTER THIRTEEN

Sees All Things As Precious: Stewardship

The Spiritual Manager is a steward. Stewards are those who care for, take responsibility for, and are accountable for assets left in their care, much like trustees.

The stewardship of a Spiritual Manager has to do with the talents and skills and resources that are entrusted to her care. In an organization, public or private, we are responsible for providing services and delivering products to our customers. We have a responsibility to see that those who have invested in us, whether it be stockholders or taxpayers, get a fair return on their investment. We have a responsibility not merely to preserve the asset but to enhance it: to grow it, to make it better, more productive, stronger, lasting.

What are some of the assets for which we will be held accountable, which we need to steward?

*   *   *

First, are our own talents. We have been given our own unique set of skills and abilities, gifts which we are expected to use for the benefit of the universe. I believe we cannot just bury those gifts but must invest them through education, learning, development, getting out in the world and trying them out, continually experimenting and learning, perhaps failing as the world deems failure, but we cannot just simply sit on them. How many times have you seen really gifted people waste those gifts? You hear the story over and over again of people who have so much potential but never fully use it.

We all know that growth is painful, that many times we have to do things we don't want to do or like to do in order to achieve personal growth. But if we really listen to ourselves and listen to the lessons that are there to be learned, we will be willing to go through that pain, that discomfort, that unpleasantness and grow. So the first area of stewardship for Spiritual Managers is clearly knowing and understanding themselves, taking the risks and going through the pain necessary to continue their own personal growth and to further use the talents and skills that they have been given.

*   *   *

The second area of stewardship involves all those skills and talents of others with which we have been entrusted. When people come to work with us they bring us so much and it is our responsibility to know and to understand all those skills and talents and to help the individual fully develop. This requires a manager who is constantly focused on knowing and understanding the unit member, and being fully committed to helping him do everything possible to grow as an individual and as a productive member in the accomplishment of the organization's vision. It takes getting out of one's self, out of your own concerns and fears and anxieties, and focusing instead on the employees and what it is that they are striving for in their life. I know that for me this is not an easy task. I still get caught up in my own fears. Part of me still worries about how I am going to look if they don't do their job. I just have to understand that's part of who I am and not let that run my life today. To really be focused on another person and to be committed to helping that person develop doesn't always mean being soft. It often means being tough. Being firm but being fair. It requires intimate knowledge of that person and what he is truly capable of, and a willingness to help him stretch to accomplish his potential.

I happen to like athletics and politics a lot. Those are two pretty competitive areas and I am always impressed by certain coaches who seem to be able to get their people to perform at their peak. Coming from Wisconsin, of course I am a Vince Lombardi fan. You may remember Fuzzy Thurston's famous quote about Coach Lombardi, "One thing about Coach Lombardi, he treats us all the same — like dogs." Tough, demanding, yet eminently fair, Coach Lombardi had the ability to make people believe in themselves because they knew he believed in them. I was there the day that Jerry Kramer drove his opponent back in that frozen tundra clearing the way for Bart Starr to dive in and beat the Dallas Cowboys for the NFL Championship. Impossible? Perhaps, but they got the job done. They were peak performers, oftentimes performing at levels beyond what they believed they were capable of, or had ever been capable of before. Coach Lombardi believed in his people and was able to help them achieve high levels of performance they had never achieved before.

In politics I have managed campaigns where we weren't supposed to have a chance. But by believing in the candidate, the vision, and the people, we were able to pull an organization together behind that vision to accomplish truly miraculous results.

Contrary to popular beliefs these days, money is not the most important ingredient in a political campaign. Belief is. Belief in the vision of the candidate and in the candidate herself. And a belief shared by hundreds or thousands of unpaid volunteers not only in the candidate and in the vision of the candidate, but that they can win. Lee Sherman Dreyfus' campaign for governor certainly was a case in point. With minuscule name recognition and no experience as a candidate, Dreyfus, president of the University of Wisconsin, Stevens Point, was able to defeat an incumbent, very well financed, Milwaukee-based congressman (who later became a U.S. Senator) in the primary and an incumbent Democrat for governor. As the second of four campaign chairs in that campaign, my contribution was to take a rag-tag bunch of dedicated college students and broaden that base into a large core of committed volunteers who not only strongly believed in the candidate and what he stood for, but saw a feasible way to become successful despite overwhelming odds. What brought about that transition?

1. Belief in the candidate and his ability. I knew in my gut he was a good, honest and capable man. His openness to his students during the Vietnam riots was symbolized by his wearing of a red vest. "If you are angry or upset," he would say, "Look for the red vest. I'm willing to listen." So the red vest became our campaign logo.

2. Belief in the campaign workers. While still students or recent graduates of the University of Wisconsin-Stevens Point, he had attracted a core of totally dedicated capable followers. All they needed was some organization, some mixing in of experienced politicos who also believed in him, a winning plan and the power to get the job done.

That's what they received from me.

3. Belief in the people, the voters. After a narrow defeat at the Republican nominating convention, we did the unthinkable, ran against the party's endorsed candidate with the slogan, "Let the people decide," and they did. One of our key strategies was to enter into a series of debates with David Carley, the democratic challenger to the incumbent governor. Dave and I had served under former Governor John Reynolds and had briefly been business associates and I had high regard for his ability and his desire to lead the state in a new direction. Both holding Ph.D.'s, Dave and Lee brought the campaign to the people by giving them good solid facts, believing they wanted substance, not images.

You see, I know it can be done. People will rise to tremendous heights led by a Spiritual Manager who believes in them, knows their skills and talents, and gives them the opportunity, in fact challenges them, to use all those skills and talents in the accomplishment of their shared vision.

*　　　　*　　　　*

The third area of stewardship has to do with the non-human resources with which we have been entrusted. Our investors' or taxpayers' money and the tools, equipment, and materials that are purchased are part of our stewardship responsibility. I mentioned earlier that the spiritual style of managing is not soft. It is not! It is and must be tough. We must make sure we are doing a good job as stewards of the resources with which we have been entrusted. We need to monitor ourselves and to hold ourselves accountable for those resources.

No one else need do it for us. We should do it for ourselves. I believe the Spiritual Manager uses the management tools available to him or her today to be able to measure how good a job is being done in the use of resources. Such techniques as benchmarking, where we observe outstanding practitioners in our field and what it is they are accomplishing with the resources they have been given. Modeling, where we create a model based on hypothetical assumptions about what we believe would be our best ways to get this job done, and then tracking the results and seeing how we are doing against that model. Going through a best practices exercise: When were we really productive, really getting the job done, really making good use of our resource? What did we do then? How did we do it? What can we learn from our own best practices that will help us to again achieve that kind of performance?

*   *   *

Of course, one thing needs to be stressed. We do not practice our stewardship in a vacuum, we are not alone. All of us, manager and members together are guided by, supported and even forgiven by our higher power. All of us as spiritual beings hold ourselves accountable to that power and want to use our resources in the way we intuit they were intended to be used. This is not the manager doing this for others. This is all of us doing this for ourselves so we will know what kind of stewards we are, always having a continuous goal of improving stewardship with the resources we have been given.

I have talked a good deal about intuition; intuiting the vision, trusting our gut, balancing our logic with our hunches, etc. This sounds really loosy-goosy, but it really isn't. It's just different for many of us because of our training and education. But it works, it really does. Let's take a look at meditation, a key element of spiritual management.

CHAPTER FOURTEEN

Seeks Inner Direction:
Meditation — The Road To Inner Power

David McClelland found most managers' dominant motivator was power, the need to be influential or to have influence. Managers like power. Moreover, they must have power if they are going to be effective. We must be able to influence others, to work with others, to move together in an agreed upon direction toward the accomplishment of our shared vision.

So the question is not do we need power but what kind of power do we need and how do we get it?

Most managers seek power externally. They want position power which gives them the formal means to reward or punish workers or the power inherent in the position itself. Because they seek these external means to power, they must constantly protect their position, defending it at all costs against invaders, whether they be from above or below. They jealously hang on to their power, refusing to listen to or to allow subordinates freedom to operate without their approval. They often resent higher levels of power when the aims or objectives of those levels are contrary to their own, and will seek through undermining and sabotaging or blocking to nullify those higher levels of power in their unit. The external road to power is fragile indeed and certainly not the best course to take.

True power comes from within the individual, not from outside.

I know that I, myself, am powerless. When I view myself in the totality of this universe I am as nothing and yet I know that I am something or I wouldn't be here. There is a place for me in this universe. That place is carrying out the will, the direction, accomplishing the purpose set for me by my higher power. That is my place. So, for me to have power, the power that will really enable me to become truly productive, I must be linked into my higher power. I must be getting some data, some information, some inkling of what it is that I am supposed to be doing if I truly want power. And I can't get that through an organizational chart.

*   *   *

Thomas Moore, psychologist and theologian, emphasizes:
> In the soul, power doesn't work the same way as it does in the ego and will. When we want to accomplish something egoistically, we gather our strength, develop a strategy, and apply every effort... The power of the soul, in contrast, is more like a great reservoir or, in traditional imagery, like the force of water in a fast-rushing river. It is natural, not manipulated, and stems from an unknown source. Our role with this kind of power is to be an attentive observer noticing how the soul wants to thrust itself into life. It is also our task to find artful means of articulating and structuring that power, taking full responsibility for it, but trusting too that the soul has intentions and necessities that we may understand only partially.[1]

Moore goes on to point out:

> One of the central difficulties involved in embarking
> on care of the soul is grasping the nature of the soul's
> discourse. The intellect works with reasons, logic,
> analysis, research, equations, and pros and cons. But
> the soul practices a different kind of math and logic.
> It presents images that are not immediately intelli-
> gible to the reasoning mind. It insinuates, offers fleet-
> ing impressions, persuades more with desire than with
> reasonableness. In order to tap the soul's power, one
> has to be conversant with its style, and watchful. The
> soul's indications are many, but they are usually ex-
> tremely subtle.[1]

Inner power, that power that comes from knowing fully, truly
who I am. Knowing my strengths and my weaknesses and being at
peace with all of that comes from being linked to my higher power.
Knowing what I am doing, what I believe in, who is truly directing
my life and this universe and that I am safe, gives me a sense of
power no one can take away from me. No reorganization, no over-
controlling, threatening boss, no disloyal, manipulative employee;
no one can take away my inner power.

So, at least for me, I agree with McClelland. I like power, I want
power, I have spent most of my life seeking power through climbing
and clawing up organizational ladders, through politics, through the
accumulation of wealth, all sorts of external means to get power. And
after I reached the top of the organizational ladder, and after I reached
the top in political clout, and after I reached financial security, I came
to the empty realization that these accomplishments did not give me

power. Power, true power, the power I was seeking, had to come from somewhere else, and that realization brought about the spiritual journey that I continue on today. I know that true power comes from myself and my relationship with God and that the road to inner power is meditation.

*   *   *

I can't pretend to tell you how to meditate. I can encourage you with everything I have to meditate.

I remember when I was in the pits of my depression during my midlife crisis and I came across a wonderful book by Jess Lair, Ph.D., called *I Don't Know Where I'm Going, But I Sure Ain't Lost.*[2] In that book he recounted his experiences with meditation and passed along many helpful hints on how to meditate. Being in such a dismal state of existence, I would try anything. So, I would faithfully get up in the morning, sit in the proper posture, practice my mantra and wait for something to happen. Well, I did that for awhile and nothing happened, and I gave up on meditation. I am not faulting Jess Lair here; I am just recounting this experience because of my own unrealistic expectations of what meditation was and how it would work for me.

Several years later, still in the pits of despair, I began to pay attention to one of the suggestions of the support group I belonged to that, if I sought through prayer and meditation to improve my conscious contact with my higher power, I would get the answers I needed. I realized I was meditating in order to get out of my misery. Using meditation as a cure-all rather than as a means of providing direction in my life didn't work for me. I still had to do the work.

What I needed was the direction. Also, I had to have confidence in myself and in the power that would come to me in the practice of meditation. You see, if I didn't believe in myself and the God within me as truly my higher power and not just an errand boy, then I would not believe what I heard. The message would go unheeded, not because of the validity of the message but because of the disbelief of the hearer.

Fortunately, a friend who had studied and practiced meditation for many years began a meditation support group. I began to meet with them at 7:00 a.m. and we would sit for 20 minutes together in silent meditation. At first I was discouraged because it seemed like my mind would never be still, constantly filled with problems of the day, or problems with a relationship or this or that or the other thing. Just constantly churning, no peace and certainly no inner message came that I could discern.

My friend told me to just relax and not fight those voices in my head. "When thoughts come to you," he said, "just relax. Acknowledge them. Greet them, and then let them go. Don't fight them. Because if you fight them, they will just get stronger in your mind." And so, I began to acknowledge the fact that my mind was not going to turn off one hundred percent. It was going to continue to do its usual mischievous stuff in wanting to be dominant in my life and wanting to direct everything. That is just the way my mind is and so I can just acknowledge that and then let it go and my inner voice can be heard.

Breathing is essential, or at least it has been for me. I must really concentrate on my breathing: deep breaths in and deep breaths out, deep breaths in and deep breaths out, and deep breaths in and deep breaths out, all the while listening to my body breathing in and breathing out. Eventually, I feel a stillness coming over me. Sometimes that lasts for seconds and other times for maybe 10 or 15 minutes. Certainly, never for the whole 20 minutes that I meditate. Like everything else I have ever done, it takes practice, just doing it over and over and over. And you will know as you meditate when you have let go of your conscious mind and allowed some higher consciousness to enter into your consciousness.

Another of the problems has to do with expectations. I expected these flashes of insight and intellectual understanding as a result of meditation. Sometimes that does happen. If I have a particular problem that I bring to meditation I might, just before I begin my meditation say, "Dear God, today, I am dealing with this," or "If it be your Will, please grant me some understanding of what it is that you will have me do today." And I begin to meditate and I can tell you that thoughts do come to me that were not there before. Clear and specific thoughts that tell me exactly what I need to do. Where do they come from? Does it really matter? I know they come and they help me tremendously.

But many times no thoughts come, no insights, no inspiration, just calm and peace. I have come to regard meditation as sort of like a computer downloading into me. It's as if I just open my ports and say, "Ok, God, dump into me today what it is that you would have me do, thoughts that you would have me think. I am just simply going to be open to these things right now." Often nothing comes to me at the time I meditate but then later on as I go through my day something will flash up, something will come to me and I will know what it is that I am supposed to do. One of the things that is really necessary is to keep a pad of paper and pencil around because those thoughts come and go in a hurry, and you need to be able to capture them because they don't necessarily come back. It is not like they are imprinted in your memory someplace so that you can just simply recall them. They come and then they are gone, and they don't seem to have a source, and they don't seem to leave any traces. So, for me at least, I need to keep a pad of paper and pencil around to jot these things down quickly.

*   *   *

So that's been my experience with meditation. There are many aids available to help you explore meditation. Some of the material I have includes an instructional tape on meditation with some meditation exercises by John Bradshaw; a tape by William Breault, S. J., *The Grace of the Present Moment: Reflections on Trust,* a CD entitled *Meditation - A Practical Survival Kit for the '90s* by Allen Holmquist, MSCC; and *Listening - How to Increase Awareness of Your Inner Guide* by Lee Coit. Other useful books are Reflections for Managers, short readings with questions to guide your meditation by Bruce Hyland and Merrill Yost, or *Meditations of Maharishi Mahesh Yogi* in which he defines meditation as "The method of drawing the attention towards the inner glory of life. A method whereby our conscious mind could explore the inner avenues of being and fathom the depths of real lasting great glories of life."[3]

Jan Kabat-Zinn's most insightful book, *Wherever You Go There You Are; Mindfulness Meditation in Everyday Life,* can really help you develop your meditation practice. He describes meditation as "not some weird cryptic activity" nor "becoming some kind of zombie, vegetable, self absorbed narcissist, navel gazer, "space cadet," cultist, devotee, mystic or Eastern philosopher. Meditation is simply about being yourself and knowing something about who that is... that you are on a path... the path that is your life... that this path we call our life has direction, that it is always unfolding..."[4]

If you need to have a better intellectual understanding of the process, I would refer you back to Willis Harman's work, and for the even more pragmatic, a book entitled *The Intuitive Manager* by Roy Roland. While this book doesn't deal with the process of meditation, it does deal extensively with its end product—that is, intuition, insight, understanding or as it is defined "knowledge gained without rational thought." Another tool, which I have not developed, is Jungian dream analysis. Here individuals are guided in focusing on their dreams as a means by which they can gain insight into their own as well as the "collective" unconscious.

*   *   *

While I have spent most of the time here talking about meditation, I don't want you to forget there is another part of the equation, that of prayer. I am really not talking about formal prayer here. I am talking about conversation with your higher power, not necessarily asking for anything but just simply providing your input into this two-way conversation. My practice is not to ask for specific things in my prayer but to simply talk to God as I would a trusted friend. If there is something I think I need, mention it, but always with a provision that if it is in accordance with God's will because I have to always remember his will is far better for me than mine. I particularly like how Gary Prather describes prayer:

> The talking does something. I pray to God, my friend,
> and it changes me, if only for a moment. I feel myself
> siding with what is good in me. I feel cleansed and I
> look around with more gentleness. Relationships ap-
> pear to reform on a new basis; the gentleness in me
> seeking the gentleness in others. I sense my own
> beauty and health and I see a core of goodness in oth-
> ers. The world dances for a moment. Now if one can
> feel it, see it, act it, and time and again has it handed
> back to him, then he knows it exists. So why am I
> fighting to leave this?[5]

*   *   *

But today I place much more emphasis on meditation, which I
see as listening to God, rather than prayer, which is talking to God.
To me meditation is my link to my higher power. To that great source
of all wisdom that exists in this universe. I know I am not the beginning and the end. I am not the one who always was, is, and always
will be. I am a spiritual being living this limited, finite life seeking my
truths and trying to the best of my ability to carry out the will of my
God. Meditation is my road map, gives me my direction, keeps me in
touch with who I am, what I need to do and where I need to go today
and for that I am eternally grateful. Don't expect too much. Don't try
too hard. Relax. Take it easy. Don't struggle and you will be amazed.
Meditation truly is the road to inner power, and inner power is the
source of all the power you need to be a Spiritual Manager.

CHAPTER FIFTEEN

Accepts Oneself While Seeking Improvement:
Practice, Not Perfection

Well, we have covered a lot of material here. Not too much of it is really new, but maybe it provides a different slant on things. Yet, even as I write this, I know I am still on a journey and I don't know for sure where the journey is taking me. All I know is that I am called to change. I am called to look at myself, to look at my behavior, to look at the reasons why I do things and to constantly assess that against a vision of the Jim I want to be… the Jim I think I am called to be. How do I know that? I have a strong feeling this Jim was not created to be the obsessed, power-driven, manipulative, dominating person I spent a good share of my life being. Maybe it is as Levinson discovered in his study of men as they go through the stages of life that I am getting in touch with that feminine part of myself, that gentle part of myself. I don't know. All I know is that today I find myself changing and being open to change. I find that it is possible to maintain my masculinity, yet at the same time see my shortcomings. Admit where I have done something that just doesn't make any sense against what it is I really want to do or be.

This chapter is called practice, not perfection. One of my favorite books is *Seat of the Soul* by physicist Gary Zukav where he continually refers to the earth school.[1] I share that sentiment. I believe I am here in this sphere, at this time, to learn things that will help me in my spiritual journey. If I stay closed and rigid; if I am defensive, blaming and avoiding, I am not going to be learning. So, I have to try to be a new person. To live a new way. This means practice. Practice, practice, practice. And with every practice, just as Deming found, I can make some progress, learn some things, change some more things and keep on going.

*   *   *

One of the obstacles is having a controlling boss yourself. What do you do if you have a controlling boss or work in an unhealthy environment and are simply not able to pull up stakes and get out? First, try to be open to leaving if necessary. If you make yourself healthy and then look for healthier opportunities, you will be amazed what comes along. There are some healthy organizations out there, just as there are some healthy people, and good organizations are always looking for more good people. However, if you are in an unhealthy, controlling environment now, then you have got to do what many bosses are called to do, be a buffer between that unhealthy controlling management and your people. You have to be the dike that keeps the ocean from engulfing your people so they have the freedom to grow, develop, and be the best they can be. It is not an easy job, but it is possible.

How can you deal with this? A couple of things, first understand that your boss can't control you. He really can't control you. People only have power over us if we decide to give them that power. If we decide not to give them the power, they don't have it. So, understand that you can make a decision not to be controlled by this person.

170

Now, how do you do that? First, do not fight the controller. Don't fight the person. This just gives power to the controller. It just gives power to the situation. Don't fight. Something I learned in politics, don't get in a spitting match with a skunk. You can't win and it will just energize the skunk. It is a funny thing about any obsession or any problem in our life, if we focus on it and fight it, we just give it power. So, you can't fight the controller. What can you do?

Rely on your higher power. Your higher power will help you reach within and find your own best self. Your own higher self. And by using your higher self, you can have sympathy for that miserable controller. Just have sympathy for him. Imagine how miserable it must be to be like that. Aren't you glad you are not like that? So have sympathy for that person. Say, "I understand, yes. I know that you have a rough job, boss. Yeah, I am really sorry for you, boss. That's tough." Have sympathy. Poor boss. But then go about your business.

Be assertive, not aggressive. Aggressive is taking the boss on, trying to get him fired, win your point, make him look bad, etc. Assertive is just quietly but firmly letting the boss know where you stand. Let him know you're not trying to get around him or change him, but that you have a right to give your input. What he does with it is his business.

Remember your boss is a human being also. Just as you have to come to know and understand and use your unit members' strengths and desires, you have to know your boss's as well. We don't just manage down, we have to manage up as well. We have to try as best we can to coach, counsel, assist our boss to be the best she can be. Remember, your power does not come from the organization, it comes through your inner being from a higher source. Use that power to help everyone in the organization fulfill the organization's mission and vision.

Stay focused on your vision. Stay focused on what it is you need to do and go about doing it. Remember the need to control others does not come from any healthy part of ourselves. Others will follow a leader who leads from high self-respect and respect for others. Controllers lack basic self regard and need to force others to do their will.

*   *   *

And how do you get all of this done? Very simple. One day at a time. I don't know of any other way to get anything done. One of my favorite cartoons, still on my refrigerator today, is Hagar the Horrible. He and his sidekick Lucky Eddie are sitting in a bar. In the first panel Hagar says, "From now on I'm going to live one day at a time." "Good idea," Eddie replies. Then in panel 2 Eddie asks, "How many have you been living?"[2]

There are so many great things to do that we get overwhelmed by them and nothing gets done. I make it a practice during my morning meditation to select a book which I read one page at a time, one day at a time. Do you know how many books I have read that way? It is amazing. This book here. If I decided I had to create this book and get it all done right now I would have never gotten it done. It is just a matter of doing something today. One day at a time.

I don't know how else to live life today except one day at a time. Yes. I have a vision, a direction today, and my life is very good. It may be different tomorrow, I don't know. I remember a very wise lady once telling me, "You know, Jim, the past is history. There is nothing you can do about it. And the future is just a guess. You have no real idea what's going to be happening tomorrow. All you have is today. Live it to the fullest. Be the best you can be today and everything else will take care of itself."

If I wait for perfection, I will never do anything. I have to accept the fact that I live life one day at a time and this is just a practice round. The only way I can learn is by doing. Planning, thinking, scheming, and plotting will not get the job done. Faith without action is dead. I believe in what I have written in this book and I try to practice it on a daily basis in all my relationships. Some days are better than others. Some relationships are easier than others. All I can do today is be open to God, my higher power. To the direction he seems to be giving to me. To the things that seem to be right in my life today and to try to do them to the best of my ability, one day at a time. He will take care of the rest.

*   *   *

How Do You Get There

I can't tell you. I know a lot of people like to have easy-to-do, one-two-three kinds of guidance but I can't tell you. I am reminded of the ancient saying, "Those who say, don't know. Those who know, don't say. You have to find it yourself." What I can tell you is what was necessary for me to go through to begin this process of moving towards spiritual management.

First and foremost was a willingness to look deeply and closely at myself, my behavior, and how my behavior affected other people. I know that when I saw my behavior clearly for the first time at that managerial grid school, I saw how it closed down other people. I used my strengths to dominate or manipulate or do whatever was necessary to get people to do what it was that I wanted them to do. I not only shut other people down but made them feel inferior. They weren't as good as I was. That was pretty clear. So, naturally, being inferior they should be willing to take my lead; in fact, they should be grateful that I was there to provide the leadership. They felt like less, so I could feel like more. But I came to acknowledge that I didn't want that in my life. Without the opportunity to closely examine myself and the impact of my behavior on others, I would have never begun to change.

Secondly, I had to be open to change. I had to do what seemed the appropriate thing in the moment and accept that I wouldn't always be right. I would make mistakes; I would sometimes appear foolish. Unfortunately, there would be times I would hurt others. But I needed to learn how to change, and that required being open, willing to take risks. I had to be willing to stumble, to fail as I understood failure, to fix my mistakes and to try again.

Third, I had to trust my gut. I am a strong "intuiter" and therefore place a great deal of confidence in my sixth sense, my ability to feel what should be done. Others may be sensors — preferring instead to rely on the tangible senses, concrete details and information. Trusting my gut allows me to remain open to possibilities within the universe. My use of logic exclusively limits me to what my brain can perceive. It cannot pick up information it has not already received and processed. Neither can it get in touch with that higher power that communicates to me through my intuitive senses. And I believe intuition is the best way to get in touch with that information and intuition works through meditation. So it may be Yung's collective unconscious or Sheldrake's morphic resonance fields or the great spirit or God or holy spirit or universal crystals or tarot cards or channels through which spirits speak, I don't know what is the best way for you to get in touch with those powers. What I do know is it is important for me to do so.

Fourth, I had to go through the pain. I honestly do not believe I would have really changed, or transformed as a friend of mine likes to say, if I had not gone through the pain. Those years starting when I was 51 until I was about 56 were hell. Sleepless nights, constant anxiety, questioning everything in my life, no sense of order, just chaos. The only way I could survive in that period was focusing on the immediate tasks that I had to do — get into graduate school, study for this exam, write this paper, and have a few close friends that I could constantly talk to (or should I say cry on their shoulders) about all the pain I was in. But gradually things fall back into place and a new life emerges. I experienced the inner change that is needed to get in touch with the universe, to be able to see all the beauty and the messages and the meaning that is there to see once I had gone through this metamorphosis.

Fifth, I had to keep the faith. Nobody promised me a rose garden and things don't flow smoothly. There will still be uncertainty. We never operate with perfect certainty in life. We slip and fall back into our old behavior. When I do this I get very discouraged, but I truly believe I am being called to some higher purpose by my higher power and I need to be steadfast in that belief and to persevere no matter what.

Sixth, remember life is a one day at a time proposition. I do not know what is going to happen in the future. All I know is right now

in this present moment. Stay in the present moment. Trust in a benevolent universe, a kindly God, a generous spirit, even as the lilies
of the field or the birds of the air.

Seventh, keep things in perspective. I am not the center of the
universe. My ego will lead me into disastrous thinking and disastrous behavior if I do not constantly remember that I am here, like
everything else that is created, to carry out the purpose of the universe. I am here to serve, not to control; I am here to benefit, not to
extort; I am here to give so that in turn I may receive.

These are just some of my thoughts. I am sure you have others.
And others in the vast spiritual literature that seems to abound around
us have many more ideas. Read it all, take it in, run it through your
own filters and see if it makes any sense to you. Bottom line, you
need to determine what it is that will work for you. Trust your gut,
trust your heart, trust your God. You will do just fine.

END NOTES

Introduction

1. Bucke, R. M., M.D. Cosmic Consciousness: *A Study in the Evolution of the Human Mind.* New York, New York: The Citadel Press, 1970. p. 2.

2. Rajneesh, B. S. *The Book.* Oregon: Rajneesh Foundation International, 1971. p. 18.

3. Maddi, S. R. *Personality Theories: A Comparative Analysis,* 4th ed., Homewood, Illinois: Darcy Press, 1980. p. 86.

4. Hawken, P., quoted in "Cosmic Business," D. P. Miller, *Yoga Journal,* March/ April, 1994. p. 68.

5. Fox, M. *The Coming of the Cosmic Christ.* San Francisco, California: Harper, 1991.

Chapter 1

1. Covey, S. R. *Seven Habits of Highly Effective People.* New York: Simon & Schuster, 1989

Chapter 2

1. *Touchstones.* New York, New York: Harper/Hazelden, 1981, July 12.

2. Morris, D. *The Naked Ape.* New York: McGraw-Hill Publishing Co., 1967. p. 147.

3. Sheehy, G. *New Passages - Mapping Your Life Across Time.* New York: Random House, 1995. pp. 420-428.

4. Rank, O., quoted in M. Fox. *The Coming of the Cosmic Christ.* San Francisco: Harper, 1991.

5. Weinberg, S. *Scientific American.* October 1994. pp. 44-49.

6. Naisbitt, J. and Aburdene, P. *Reinventing the Corporation: Transforming Your Job and Your Company, The New Information Society.* New York: Warner Books, 1985. p. 69.

7. Orsborn, C. *Inner Excellence: Spiritual Principles of Life-Given Business.* San Rafael, California: The New World Library, 1992. p. 13.

8. Harmon, W. *Insight into the New Age.* San Francisco: Institute of Noetic Sciences, 1988.

9. Orsborn, C. *Inner Excellence,* p. 6.

10. James, G. *Business Wisdom of the Electronic Elite.* New York: Times Books, 1996.

11. Riley, M. *Corporate Healing: Solutions to the Impact of the Addictive Personality in the Workpace.* Deerfield Beach, Florida: Health Communications, Inc., 1990. p. 8.

12. Chappell, T. *The Soul of a Business.* New York: Bantam Doubleday Dell Audio, 1993.

Chapter 3

1. Swartz, S. *Godspell.* New Cadenza Music Corp., ASCAP, 1973.

2. Sheehy, G. *Passages, Predictable Crises of Adult Life.* New York: E. P. Dutton & Co., Inc., 1974. p. 45.

Chapter 4

1. *Tallahassee Democrat,* Wednesday, May 29, 1996.

2. Lewis, C. S. *The Inspirational Writings of C. S. Lewis.* New York: Inspirational Press, 1994. p. 382.

3. *Answers in the Heart.* San Francisco: Harper & Row, 1989. p. May 31.

4. *Touchstones.* New York: Harper/Hazeldon, 1987. p. May 31.

5. *Manual for Teachers: A Course in Miracles.* Glen Ellen, California: Foundation for Inner Peace, 1992. p. 40.

6. Chopra, D. *Seven Spiritual Laws of Success: A Practical Guide to the Fulfillment of Your Dreams.* San Rafael, California: New World Library, 1994. p. 62.

Chapter 5

1. Rodegast, P. and Stanton, J. *Emmanuel's Book: A Manual for Living Comfortable in the Cosmos.* New York: Bantam Books, 1987. p. 124.

2. Senge, P. M. *The Fifth Discipline: Building Shared Vision.* New York: Doubleday,1990. pp. 203-232.

3. Naisbitt, J. and Aburdene, P. *Reinventing the Corporation: Transforming Your Job and Your Company.* New York: The New Information Society, Warner Books, 1985. pp. 20-21.

4. Thoreau, H. D. *Walden: A Life in the Woods.* New York: Anchor Books, 1973. p. 272.

5. Burkett, L. *Business by the Book: The Complete Guide of Biblical Principles for Business Men and Women.* Nashville, Tennessee: Thomas Nelson Publishers, 1990. pp. 110 and 124.

6. Messing, B. *The Tao on Management.* Los Angeles, California: Audio Renassaince Tapes, Inc., 1989.

7. Peters, T. J. and Waterman, Jr., R. H. *In Search of Excellence: Lessons from America's Best Run Companies.* New York: Warner Books, 1982.

Chapter 6

1. Covey, S. R. *Principle-Centered Leadership.* New York: Fireside,1992, p. 155.

2. Peters, T. *The Tom Peters Seminar, Crazy Times Call for Crazy Organizations.* New York: Vintage Books, 1994. p. 30.

3. Serwer, A. E. *Lessons from America's Fastest Growing Companies.* Fortune Magazine, August 8, 1994, p. 50.

4. Walton, S., with J. Huey. *Made in America - My Story.* New York: Doubleday, 1992. p. 217.

5. Peters, T. *Liberation Management.* New York: Alfred A. Knopf, Inc., 1992. pp. 238, 239, 245.

6. Belaseo, J. and Stayer, R. *Flight of the Buffalo: Soaring to Excellence, Learning to Let Employees Lead:* New York: Warner Books, 1993.

7. Toffler, I. *Power Shift: Knowledge, Wealth and Violence at the Edge of the 21st Century.* New York: Bantam Books,1990. pp. 204-217.

8. Osborne, D. and Gaebler, T. *Reinventing Government: How the Entrepreneural Spirit is Transforming the Public Sector.* Reading, Ma.: Addison-Wesley Publishing Co., 1992.

Chapter 7

1. McGregor, D. *The Human Side of Enterprise.* New York: McGraw-Hill, 1961.

2. Robinson, A. J. *Level III Manual.* Tallahassee, Florida: Florida Center for Public Management, 1994. p. 3.1.13.

3. Barker, J. *The Business of Paradigms.* Discovering the Future Series Video. Chart House International, 1989.

4. Zukav, G. *The Seat of the Soul.* New York: Fireside, 1990. p. 118.

5. Autry, J. *Love and Profit: The Art of Caring Leadership.* New York, New York: William Morrow & Co., Inc.,1991. p. 122.

6. Cornford, F. M. *The Republic of Plato.* London: Oxford University Press, 1945. p. 318.

7. Covey, S. R. *Principle-Centered Leadership.* New York: Fireside, 1992. pp. 33-39.

8. Waitley, D. *Empires of the Mind: Lessons to Lead and Succeed in a Knowledge-based World.* New York: William Morrow & Co., Inc., 1995. p. 4.

Chapter 8

1. Kouzes, J. M. and Posner, B. Z. *Creditability: How Leaders Gain and Lose It, Why People Demand It.* San Francisco, California: Josey-Bass, 1993, Forward.

2. Champy, J. *Reingineering Management: The Mandate for New Leadership.* New York: Harper Business, 1995. pp. 204-205.

3. Fomm, B. *The Ten Commandments of Business and How to Break Them.* Chicago, Illinois: Nightingale Conate Audio,1991.

4. Champy, J. *Reengineering Management.*

5. Covey, S. R. *Principle-Centered Leadership.* New York: Fireside, 1992. p. 34.

6. de Saint Exupery, A. *The Little Prince.* San Diego, California: Harcourt Brace Jovanovich. pp. 87-88.

7. Waitley, D. *Empires of the Mind: Lessons to Lead and Succeed in a Knowledge-based World.* New York, New York: William Morrow & Co., Inc., 1995. p. 4.

8. I have heard this quote attributable to Bennis but in looking through his significant contribution to the leadership literature I have been unable to locate a specific cite. Nonetheless, I have chosen to include it here because of the substantial evidence I see of this philosophy being carried out in the students in my class who are also currently serving in the military, in particular those who served in the Gulf War. Also see Creech, W. *The Five Pillars of TQM: How to Make Total Quality Management Work For You.* New York: Truman Talley Books, 1994

9. Kouzes, J. M. and Posner, B. Z. *The Leadership Challenge - How To Get Extraordinary Things Done in Organizations.* San Francisco: Jossey-Bass, 1987. pp. 163, 164.

10. de Pree, M. *Leadership Jazz.* New York: Bantam Audio, 1992.

11. Greenleaf, R. K. *The Private Writings of, On Becoming a Servant Leader,* edited by Don M. Frick and Larry C. Spears. San Francisco, California: Jossey-Bass, 1986. pp. 1, 2.

12. Peters, T. *Thriving on Chaos: Handbook for a Management Revolution.* New York: Harper and Row,1988. pp. 601, 603.

13. *Good News: The New Testament in Today's English,* 4th ed. New York: American Bible Society,1976.

14. Rogers, R. W. *The Psychological Contract of Trust: Trust Development in the 90's Workplace.* Development Dimensions International, 1994. pp. 12, 13.

15. de Pree, M. *Leadership Jazz.* New York: Bantam Audio,1992. Also book form by Dell Publishing, New York, 1992.

16. *Tallahassee Democrat,* May 28, 1996. p. 11a.

17. Breton, D. and Largent, C. *The Soul of Economies: Spiritual Evolution Goes to the Marketplace.* Wilmington, Delaware: Idea House Publishing Company,1991. pp. 9-25.

18. Peck, S., M.D. *A World Waiting to Be Born: Civility Rediscovered.* New York: Bantam Books, 1994. p. 245.

Chapter 9

1. Heider,J. *The Tao of Leadership: Leadership Strategies for a New Age.* New York: Bantam Books, 1986. p. 127.

2. I have read and used so much literature on W. Edwards Deming I have no idea where this information comes from specifically. One book you may want to read is by A. Gabor, *The Man Who Discovered Quality: How W. Edwards Deming Brought the Quality Revolution to America: The Stories of Ford,* Times Books, New York, New York, 1990.

3. Rogers, R. W. *The Psychological Contract of Trust: Trust Development in the 90's Workplace.* Development Dimensions International, 1994. pp. 12, 13.

Chapter 10

1. Peters,T. *Liberation Management, Necessary Disorganization for the Nano Second Nineties.* New York: Alfred A. Knopf, 1992. pp. 238-242.

2. Toffler, I. *Power Shift: Knowledge, Wealth and Violence at the Edge of the 21st Century.* New York: Bantam Books, 1990. p. 205.

3. Fisher, L. *Gandhi: His Life and Message for the World.* Mentor Books, 1954, p. 35.

4. Ban, C. CPM article.

Chapter 11

1. Forthomme, C. *Conversational Consultants: Organizational Development and Transformation.* Barbara Woodson-Shepard, AHP Perspective, April, 1988, p. 5.

2. Flynn, B. *Conversational Consultants: Organizational Development and Transformation.* Barbara Woodson-Shepard, AHP Perspective, April, 1988, p. 4.

3. Drucker, P. *The Coming of the New Organization.* Harvard Business Review, January/February, 1988, pp. 45-53.

4. Kortals, S. "Bobby McFerrin: The Multitalented Maestro." *The Aspen Times,* Friday, July 12, 1996, p. 26b.

5. Sinetar, M. *Work as a Spiritual Path: How to Bring Joy and Meaning to Your Work Life.* Boulder, Colorado: Sounds True Recordings, 1992.

Chapter 12

1. While there is a wealth of information including several separate texts of these three founders of motivational theory, a nice summary can be found in F. S. Hill's, *Compensation Decision Making,* Chicago: The Dragon Press, 1987, pp. 24-28.

2. Kouzes, J. M. and Posner, B. Z. *The Leadership Challenge - How To Get Extraordinary Things Done in Organizations.* San Francisco, California: Jossey-Bass, 1987. pp. 163, 164.

3. Farson, R. *Management of the Absurd: Paradoxes of Leadership.* New York: Simon and Schuster Audio,1996.

4. May, R. *Power and Innocence: A Search for the Source of Violence,* 1st ed. New York, New York: Norton, 1972.

Chapter 14

1. Moore, T. *The Care of the Soul.* New York: Harper Perennial, 1994. pp. 119-122.

2. Lair, J., Ph.D. *I Don't Know Where I'm Goin' But I Sure Ain't Lost.* New York: Fawcett Crest,1984.

3. Yogi, M. M. *Meditations of Maharishi Mahesh Yogi.* New York: Bantam Books, Inc., 1968.

4. Kabat-Zinn, J. *Wherever You Go There You Are; Mindfulness Meditation in Everyday Life.* New York: Hyperion, 1994.

5. Prather, H. *Notes on Love and Courage.* Garden City, NY: Doubleday & Company, 1977.

Chapter 15

1. Zukav, G. *The Seat of the Soul.* New York: Fireside,1990. p. 118.

2. Browne, C. "Hagar the Horrible," *Tallahassee Democrat,* February 12, 1989.

"...be concerned above everything else with the Kingdom of God and with what he requires of you, and he will provide you with all these other things."

Matthew 6:33

About Jim McMichael

Has been a Senior Management Trainer for Florida State University since 1989, consistently receiving outstanding ratings from his manager-students. Hear what some of his fellow managers have to say about Jim:

"Dynamic instructors are few and far between. Thank you for being one."

"One of the better courses and instructors I have ever had."

"He did not give us all the answers but allowed us to find them within ourselves."

"Well worth the time and money."

"It is evident that he has vast knowledge and experience in management."

"He cares for each person's concern and is honest."

"I enjoyed Jim's reflection on personal experiences. What a great way to make "abstract" concepts have real meaning."

Now you can share in Jim's exceptional ability to make abstract management concepts real and usable in everyday life in *The Spiritual Style of Management: Who is Running this Show Anyway?*

- Has held senior management positions as President, Unionmutual Management Corporation, Executive Director, Wisconsin State Commission on Aging, and business owner.

- Highly regarded. Advisor to four national administrations, named one of Wisconsin's Five Outstanding Young Men and one of the Outstanding Young Men of America, and Wisconsin's State Employee of the Year.

- Innovator. Helped develop Meals on Wheels, Circuit Breaker Tax Legislation, early financial planner cited in *Money* magazine.

- Consultant and Speaker.

With his wife Eileen, Jim shares seven children and a miniature schnauzer, Baby. Living near the quaint village of Havana, Florida on the North Florida Art Trail, he spends his time teaching, consulting, and writing. Every day is anchored with his meditation practice and the perspective he has gained in working his spiritual program. For this, he thanks God and those who carried the message.